SOLVING YOUR PERSONAL PROBLEMS

PETER HONEY is a psychologist and management consultant who specializes in helping people, both at work and in their personal life, to better their relationships. He is a member of the Institute of Management Consultants, the British Psychological Society and the Association of Teachers of Management, and has written numerous articles for training journals as well as appearing on television and radio. His other books include *Face-to-Face* and *Solving People Problems*, and he is co-author of *Developing Interactive Skills*. Born in 1937, he lives in Berkshire, and is married with three children.

Overcoming Common Problems Series

The ABC of Eating
JOY MELVILLE

Arthritis
Is your suffering really necessary?
DR WILLIAM FOX

Birth Over Thirty
SHEILA KITZINGER

Calm Down
How to cope with frustration and anger
DR PAUL HAUCK

Depression
Why it happens and how to overcome it
DR PAUL HAUCK

Divorce and Separation
ANGELA WILLANS

Enjoying Motherhood
How to have a happy pregnancy
DR BRICE PITT

Epilepsy Handbook
SHELAGH McGOVERN

Fears and Phobias
What they are and how to overcome them
DR TONY WHITEHEAD

Feeling Healthy
How to stop worrying about your health
DR F E KENYON

Fight Your Phobia and Win!
DAVID LEWIS

Flying Without Fear
TESSA DUCKWORTH AND DAVID MILLER

Guilt
Why it happens and how to overcome it
DR VERNON COLEMAN

Herpes: What to do when you have it
DR OSCAR GILLESPIE

How to Bring Up Your Child Successfully
DR PAUL HAUCK

How to Control your Drinking
DRS MILLER & MUNOZ

How to Cope with Stress
DR PETER TYRER

How to Cope with your Nerves
DR TONY LAKE

How to do what you want to Do
DR PAUL HAUCK

How to Love and be Loved
DR PAUL HAUCK

How to Sleep Better
DR PETER TYRER

How to Stand up for Yourself
DR PAUL HAUCK

Jealousy
Why it happens and how to overcome it
DR PAUL HAUCK

Loneliness
DR TONY LAKE

Making Marriage Work
DR PAUL HAUCK

Making the Most of Middle Age
DR BRICE PITT

Meeting People is Fun
How to overcome shyness
DR PHYLLIS SHAW

No More Headaches
LILIAN ROWEN

One Parent Families
A practical guide to coping
DIANA DAVENPORT

Overcoming Tension
DR KENNETH HAMBLY

Self-help for your Arthritis
EDNA PEMBLE

The Sex Atlas
DR ERWIN HAEBERLE

Six Weeks to a Healthy Back
ALEXANDER MELLEBY

Solving Your Personal Problems
PETER HONEY

Stress and Your Stomach
DR VERNON COLEMAN

Successful Sex
DR F E KENYON

What Everyone Should Know About Drugs
KENNETH LEECH

Why be Afraid?
How to overcome your fears
DR PAUL HAUCK

Overcoming Common Problems

SOLVING
YOUR PERSONAL PROBLEMS

Peter Honey

SHELDON PRESS
LONDON

First published in Great Britain in 1983 by
Sheldon Press, SPCK, Marylebone Road, London NW1 4DU

British Library Cataloguing in Publication Data

Honey, Peter
    Solving your personal problems.–(Overcoming common problems)
    1. Behaviour modification
    I. Title   II. Series
    153.8'5   BF637.B4

    ISBN 0-85969-389-9
    ISBN 0-85969-390-2 Pbk

Typeset by Inforum Ltd, Portsmouth
Printed in Great Britain by
Richard Clay (The Chaucer Press) Ltd
Bungay, Suffolk

Contents

1

What are Personal Problems?

Personal problems come in all sorts of shapes and sizes. They can be trivial or serious, amusing or tragic, expected or unexpected, temporary or persistent, private or shared. Life is littered with personal problems. Pick up any newspaper or magazine and you'll find it packed with personal problems of one sort or another; medical problems, health problems, appearance problems, career problems, legal problems, financial problems, relationship problems, emotional problems, and the so-called 'psychological' problems.

In this book we are going to focus on how to solve problems that arise in our relationships with other people. The problems may occur in our immediate family with spouses or children, or in our extended families with relatives and in-laws, or in our neighbourhood with friends and acquaintances, or at work with bosses or colleagues. You know the sort of thing. Husbands who drive you scatty when they come in later than they promised without any sort of apology or explanation. Wives who irritate you with nagging about things that seem (to you) inconsequential. Children who don't keep their things tidy and expect to be waited on hand and foot. Friends who make catty remarks and try to belittle you. Neighbours who complain about the noise. Bosses who don't keep you in the picture and make unreasonable demands. Or the problems might be more serious with cruelty, violence, addiction, vandalism, or dishonesty involved.

Whatever the problems are and whoever they are with, one thing is certain: there are a lot of them about! To find out just how much, I recently conducted an informal survey by eavesdropping on conversations in pubs, restaurants, launderettes, and other places where people have voluntary exchanges. I found that more than 70 per cent of the conversations were about personal problems in relationships with other people. Conversations

1

about sport came next, with motor cars and politics after that!

What is a personal problem?

Personal problems are hard to pinpoint very precisely because so much depends on the eye of the beholder. A major problem for one person is a minor irritation to another. A problem that overwhelms one person is accepted as an interesting challenge by another. Let's start by being more precise about what a problem, any sort of problem, is.

Probably the easiest way to think of a problem is to imagine it as a gap. The gap is the difference between what you've got and what you want. If you have got a partner who constantly criticizes you and you want a partner who constantly praises you then you've got a gap, or, in other words, a problem. Sometimes the gap is small, in which case you can probably see an obvious way to bridge it; other gaps are vast and stop us dead in our tracks.

If a problem is the difference between what you've got and what you want, what is a *personal* problem? *It is a problem that belongs to you*. This concept of a problem *belonging* to you may, at first, seem strange because there is an understandable tendency to blame other people for our problems. If your husband comes in late surely it's his fault? In this you might be right, but notice that his behaviour is giving *you* a problem. You are the one with a gap between what you've got (a husband coming home late) and what you want (a husband who is punctual).

This concept of *owning* problems is important because if we are not clear who the problem belongs to it will prevent us from taking appropriate action. We may, for example, sit around convinced that it is up to other people to do something, or assume responsibility for other people's problems, convinced that they are ours, not theirs.

Another important feature of personal problems is that they develop gradually over a period of time. They slip, almost imperceptibly, into being. At first they are insignificant, only gradually

2

over weeks, months or even years, developing into significant personal problems. It's rather like a wedge. At the thin end the problems aren't worth bothering about. It's only when we get to the thick end that the problems seem pressing, even desperate. With hindsight, it's easy to look back down the slope of the wedge and see the action we should have taken, and could so easily have taken, at some earlier stage.

In this book we are concerned with how to solve personal problems at the thick end of the wedge: problems with people that have developed over a period of time until they have settled down obstinately into a depressing permanence.

How good are you at solving personal problems?

During your lifetime you are rarely free of personal problems of one sort or another. As soon as one problem goes it is replaced by another. As Oscar Wilde remarked, 'Life is just one thing after another.' There may be temporary respites but it is unrealistic to expect a total absence of personal problems for long. What matters is how we deal with them and that's exactly what this book should help you to do more successfully.

Are you a successful problem solver? Find out by running through the checklist of thirty items that follows. All the items are paired. Simply tick the appropriate box to indicate which statement you agree with. Whenever you are not sure, leave both boxes blank. The checklist items are in random order, so please do not assume any order of importance. For best results complete the questionnaire as honestly as you can rather than merely ticking the statement you think is right.

How to score your questionnaire

Of the thirty items in the checklist, half probe your beliefs and half your actions. The first thing you need to do is 'unscramble' the questionnaire by indicating which boxes you ticked and totalling up the resultant score.

1. When I've got a problem with someone I try to see what I did to cause it.   A □   B □   When I've got a problem with someone I blame them for causing it.

2. In my opinion people's actions are largely governed by their personality make-up.   A □   B □   In my opinion people's actions are largely governed by what happens to them.

3. I readily accept that I need to change myself in order to improve the reactions of other people.   A □   B □   Quite honestly, I think other people need to change to fall in line with me.

4. I rarely show sympathy for other people.   A □   B □   I often say things like 'I understand how you must feel . . .'

5. I maintain that people acquire most of their characteristic ways.   A □   B □   I maintain that people inherit most of their characteristic ways.

6. I often ask for outside help when I've got a problem to solve.   A □   B □   I much prefer to keep my problems to myself.

7. I refuse to accept that any problem is insoluble.   A □   B □   I'm convinced that some problems are impossible to solve.

8. When I've got a personal problem, I tend to get steamed up and emotional about it.   A □   B □   When I've got a personal problem, I like to think it over rationally.

9. When I've got a problem with someone they are likely to be the last to know.   A □   B □   When I've got a problem with someone likely as not I'll tell them so.

10. I maintain it is best to shrug off personal problems.   A □   B □   I maintain it is best to face personal problems squarely.

4

	A	B	
11 The bigger the problem, the more I try to break it down into manageable bits.	A	B	The bigger the problem, the more I feel overwhelmed and uncertain where to make a start.
12 I like to trace a personal problem back to its origins.	A	B	I concentrate on understanding the problem in the 'here-and-now'.
13 If things don't work out, I feel dejected and tend to give up.	A	B	If things don't work out, I go back to square one and start all over again.
14 Other people cause me problems.	A	B	I cause my own problems.
15 I keep my personal problems to myself.	A	B	I openly admit to having personal problems.
16 I don't expect people to change as a result of being told that they should.	A	B	I expect people to change after I have had a go at them.
17 I believe that people tend to adopt behaviour patterns that get them what they want.	A	B	I reckon people are unpredictable and react spontaneously as the mood takes them.
18 I'm always expecting to find ready-made solutions.	A	B	I believe each problem is unique and needs its own tailor-made solution.
19 I'm often accused of putting my foot in it and unnecessarily upsetting other people.	A	B	I'm careful to trim my behaviour so that it is appropriate to those I am with.
20 I like to experiment with new or different ways of doing things.	A	B	I prefer to stick to my normal way of doing things.
21 When personal problems crop up they always seem to catch me unawares.	A	B	When personal problems crop up I accept them as inevitable.
22 I believe my head should rule my heart.	A	B	I believe my heart should rule my head.

23 People have to accept me as they find me — like it or lump it.　　A　B　I constantly monitor the effect my behaviour is having on other people.

24 I'm convinced that the best way to change people's behaviour is to change their underlying attitudes.　　A　B　I reckon the best way to change people's behaviour is to change the events that surround it.

25 There is no point in planning because I chop and change as the mood takes me.　　A　B　I find that a thought-through plan helps me to be consistent.

26 In my enthusiasm I often set off with the best of intentions only to find I was too ambitious.　　A　B　I'm careful to be realistic and check that a solution to a problem is feasible before committing myself to it.

27 When it comes to solving entrenched personal problems, I expect the result to be gradual.　　A　B　When it comes to solving entrenched personal problems, I expect immediate improvements.

28 When I'm being candid with someone who has caused me a problem, I usually strike while the iron is hot (i.e. when the problem occurs).　　A　B　When I'm being candid with someone who has caused me a problem I usually choose a time after the incident when they are likely to be more receptive.

29 When I've got a personal problem, I believe it is best to take some initiative to prevent the problem developing.　　A　B　When I've got a personal problem, I think it is best to delay and see if the problem blows over.

30 When people behave in ways that disappoint me, I try to speculate about their underlying motives, attitides, and feelings.　　A　B　When people behave in ways that disappoint me, I try to identify what circumstances brought about their behaviour.

6

BELIEFS			ACTIONS		
ITEM	POINTS		ITEM	POINTS	
	A	B		A	B
2	0	1	1	1	0
3	1	0	4	0	1
5	1	0	6	1	0
7	1	0	8	0	1
9	0	1	10	0	1
13	0	1	11	1	0
14	0	1	12	0	1
16	1	0	15	0	1
17	1	0	19	0	1
18	0	1	21	0	1
20	1	0	23	0	1
22	1	0	25	0	1
24	0	1	26	0	1
27	1	0	28	0	1
29	1	0	30	0	1
	TOTAL	8		TOTAL	4

The interpretation of your questionnaire scores is overleaf on page 8.

Portrait of successful problem solvers

Just to give you a taste of things to come here is an identikit picture of what successful problem solvers are like. The description that follows is supposed, by the way, to intrigue you, not to worry you. It is to inspire you to continue reading this book, and not designed to make you feel inadequate!

One of the first things you'd notice about successful problem solvers is how alert they are to personal problems. They readily

Beliefs	Actions	Interpretation
less than 5	less than 5	You have a long way to go before becoming a successful problem solver. This book will show you how!
5 - 10	5 - 10	You are already moderately good at solving personal problems. This book will help you to be even better!
11 - 15	11 - 15	You are already a competent problem solver.
less than 5	11 - 15	Your techniques are good but you need to improve your grasp of the principles.
11 - 15	less than 5	You've got the principles straight but you need to improve on your techniques.
5 - 10	11 - 15	You only need to polish up on the principles.
11 - 15	5 - 10	You only need to make some minor adjustments to your technique.

admit to having personal problems of their own and have an uncanny knack of sensing problems that are troubling people they meet. When they describe their personal problems they do so in a succinct, almost matter-of-fact way. They are not soppy or sentimental or defeatist. They do not grumble or attribute blame. Instead they acknowledge their ownership of the problem and accept full responsibility for doing something about it. If you tell them about a problem which is troubling you – and this is highly likely since they are the sort of people you find it easy to talk to – they listen more than they talk. They ask questions about your problem that get to the heart of the matter and, even though they haven't told you what to do, you emerge clearer and resolved to tackle the problem. If they offer advice, they do so in a non-interfering, take-it-or-leave-it way. By no stretch of the imagination are they busybodies or do-gooders.

They accept, in a passive yet positive way, the inevitability of personal problems and expect no more than brief respites between problems. They obviously don't welcome personal problems but neither do they dread them. This mature stance helps them to detect problems at an early stage – well before reaching a crisis point at the thick-end-of-the-wedge. Once they have spotted a personal problem they do not procrastinate, hoping the problem will go away of its own accord. Neither do they leap into some piece of ill-considered action. Instead they think about the problem and how best to tackle it. If they decide to confess their problem to someone they put some effort into being clear whether they want sympathy, guidance, or counselling. If they feel out of their depth they do not hesitate to track down appropriate professional help. In doing so they harbour no illusions about perfect answers and resist the temptation to shift the responsibility for their problem on to an expert.

Healthy optimism is an outstanding characteristic of successful problem solvers. They refuse to let personal problems get them down. They don't exactly thrive on problems but when they occur they certainly view them as challenges and refuse to accept that any problem, however worrying or apparently hopelessly difficult, is insoluble. They believe that problems are there to be solved and that they have not just one, but many possible courses of action open to them.

Their optimism stems from two basic assumptions. First, they believe that human behaviour is caused as much by external events as by internal personality factors. Second, they believe that changes in external events will inevitably result in changes in behaviour.

Successful problem solvers are confident that a thorough examination of the immediate events surrounding a behaviour pattern will be sufficiently revealing to give them lots of ideas about how to change the behaviour in question. They are happy to apply the same systematic approach to change their own behaviour and fully acknowledge that they must change themselves in order to bring about beneficial changes in other people. They resist the temptation to make sweeping generalizations about people or to label personality types. Instead, they put effort into accurately observing how people are actually behaving, fully accepting and respecting differences between people. They are also preoccupied with examining what is happening now rather than being dragged backwards into past history.

Successful problem solvers are extraordinarily open not just about their problems but also about their tactics. They go out of their way to 'grasp the nettle' and to be honest with people, without judging them, in a way that doesn't cause offence. They are careful to help people to see the benefits of making changes and wary of the dangers of exploitation and manipulation.

Read on to find out how you can become a successful problem solver!

2

Different Ways of Approach

Later in this book I shall introduce you to a problem-solving technique that specializes in analysing and solving personal problems. The technique is quite likely to be new to you. It certainly strikes most people as novel. Meanwhile, in order to see the need for a different approach, let's review the things that people usually do (and don't do) when they are faced with personal problems.

As we shall see, some of the approaches are *not* recommended and others are worth trying. I simply want to set the scene for the new approach so that we can see how it supplements things you might already be doing.

Do nothing and hope it will go away

Alas, this is a widespread reaction to personal problems. It is because so many of us are ostriches that personal problems are allowed to fester and grow until, suddenly, we find ourselves at the thick end of the wedge.

There are many reasons why the temptation to put things off is so strong. Doing something, as opposed to doing nothing, involves risk, and taking a risk requires courage. How *much* courage depends on the magnitude of the risk of course but, inevitably, courage is involved. We have to steel ourselves to forsake what is familiar and to face the unknown.

Sticking doggedly to the familiar, personal problems and all, is a perfectly understandable reaction. It's our way of avoiding the uncertainty of taking action or doing something different. Being in a state of uncertainty is psychologically uncomfortable and it's predictable that we'll either avoid it, by taking no action or, whether we take action or not, achieve psychological comfort by insisting that we did the right thing. This tendency to rationalize

11

is an important psychological protector. The story is told of a small religious sect who were convinced that God was going to destroy the world. They claimed to know the date and time when this was going to happen and took the risk of forecasting this publicly. No one took much notice, except to ridicule them. On the day in question they gathered together to prepare for the end of the world. The designated time came and went, and nothing happened. This threw them into a state of psychological discomfort. They had stuck their necks out, made a public prediction, been ridiculed for it, and got it wrong. After some hours of mulling over what to do they hit on the perfect rationalization. They realized that their faith and prayers had saved the world and persuaded God to postpone (perhaps even cancel?) its ending. Psychological comfort was restored and the experience left them even more resolute that they were right.

Another reason why we often opt to do nothing when faced with a personal problem is that there is always a chance that, if we wait, something will happen to resolve the situation. I expect you can remember times when your procrastination paid off because someone else took the initiative while you were still thinking about it. This happens to me quite frequently when I draw up a weekly, or daily, list of things to do. Often I hesitate to phone someone, or to organize something, even though it's on my list and, lo and behold, they contact me, thus saving me the effort and reducing my telephone bill! It's also very satisfying to cross things off my list as 'done' even though I didn't, in fact, do anything.

Much the same can happen with personal problems. Things do sometimes happen fortuitously, and circumstances do change, without us necessarily having to take action. The more this happens, the more our tendency to wait and see is reinforced and the more likely we are to repeat it.

Unfortunately, even though doing nothing is so understandable, and so popular, it often only succeeds in allowing personal problems to get worse rather than better. We saw earlier how personal problems often develop gradually in tiny steps. Putting

12

things off gives the problem time to grow, from something relatively minor and easy to correct, to something major and difficult to tackle. The irony is that the more substantial the problem, the more risk is involved in doing something about it and, therefore, the more likely we are to do nothing. This is the first of many vicious circles that we will meet as we analyse personal problems in more depth.

So, doing nothing, even though it can turn out well by chance, is not recommended as a particularly worthwhile approach. However, it is worth remembering that 'doing nothing' is always an option to be considered alongside other alternatives.

Discount the problem

We discount personal problems whenever we convince ourselves that they aren't really very important. It is easy to feel that we are making a mountain out of a molehill. After all, doesn't everyone have their fair share of personal problems? What's the point of making a fuss?

In a sense, discounting personal problems is another way of trying to become psychologically comfortable. Obviously, if the problem is nothing more than a minor irritation it's easier to decide to do nothing. There are always plenty of excuses preventing us from taking action. We don't want to upset people. 'Now isn't the time. I'll raise it if they do it again.' I remember one experience we had with a French au pair girl. My wife was confined to bed with a slipped disc and, with three young children, we were extraordinarily dependent on Lizzy. In the upheaval she wasn't told what to do as thoroughly as she should have been and, after a couple of weeks, the trail of wreckage had to be seen to be believed. Some ten years later our house still bears scars from that era. She forgot to turn the iron off and it burnt through the ironing board. She left a plastic bowl too close to the grill and it melted. She slammed a door so hard the glass shattered. She stuck posters up in her newly decorated room with sellotape and, when they came down, so did the wallpaper.

Incident by incident we discounted the problems. We rational-ized that she'd soon settle down, soon find her feet. In any case we didn't want to upset her and, in our circumstances at the time, we didn't want to risk having to find a replacement. Gradually the problem escalated, moving up the wedge from irritating to frustrating. The atmosphere was tense. Finally the au pair did something – we can't remember what – that pushed us over the edge. I decided to sit down and do the decent thing by drawing up a very precise job description. In it I spelled out all her respon-sibilities with such precision that there could, no longer, be any doubt about her duties and the standards we expected her to attain. With the document painstakingly drawn up – it ran to some pages and took me hours – I summoned her to my study and asked her to read it. To my horror she read a few lines and flew into a rage, tearing the precious document to shreds!

My mistake had been to discount the problem, pretending that all the mishaps were trivial, and then to over-react once the discounting stopped.

Discounting problems, particularly problems with people, is a common practice not just at home but also at work and in politics. Problems of discontent are belittled until they escalate into strikes or riots. Everyone knows that when people strike it is an expression of frustration that has built up over a long period of time. One hundred and one incidents, each discounted as insig-nificant at the time, grow until the one hundred and second incident acts like the straw that broke the camel's back.

All the evidence suggests that discounting problems is not an efficient way of dealing with them. Not only does the discounting give time for small problems to grow into big ones but the actual act of belittling personal problems tends to aggravate the situa-tion. Can you recall how small you felt when, having admitted to a problem, someone said, 'Oh, that's no problem' or 'Can't see what your problem is. It's obvious that you should do so and so'. In effect, these responses amount to discounts. Your problem is described as no problem. The solution is obvious. Both you and your problem have been dismissed as negligible. The chances are

14

that you won't appreciate this treatment and, depending on how you react to these snubs, matters become a little worse.

Keep it to yourself and worry about it

There are really *two* approaches here, but they so frequently go hand in hand that it is best to consider them together.

There may be many reasons for keeping a personal problem to yourself. It may be that there isn't anyone handy, or acceptable, to share it with. The problem itself may be so intimate that you may be too embarrassed or inhibited to describe it to anyone. Or it may be that you feel so emotional and confused about the problem that you can't find the words to express it.

Of course, another reason for keeping it to yourself is that you may have been brought up to believe in the 'stiff upper lip' stance. Many people feel that admitting to personal problems is really an admission of their inadequacy rather than anything else. Interestingly, the reverse is usually the case: being open about personal problems is a sign of strength rather than of weakness. Having bottled up a problem, perhaps for a long period, it is often a surprise to find people admiring your honesty in declaring it, and an even bigger surprise to find that other people have similar problems to your own.

Bottling up your problems doesn't necessarily mean that you will worry about them (any more than declaring them will mean that you will stop worring about them), but the two often go together. Worrying is such a common reaction to personal problems that we tend to think it natural and inevitable.

The fascinating thing about worrying is that even as we do it we know it is pointless. We don't need anyone to tell us 'There's no point in worrying about it', because intellectually we know this already. This discrepancy between knowing one thing and doing another is common in human behaviour and reminds us that intellect and emotions often operate independently of each other. Despite the fact that most people acknowledge that worrying doesn't solve anything, it is still a widespread reaction to personal problems.

The reasons why people worry are varied and complex but a frequent attraction is that since worrying takes up time and energy it gives us the illusion that we are doing something. Since we all know that we should do something rather than nothing in the face of personal problems this is yet another way to feel psychologically more comfortable.

At first sight this seems ridiculous. Few people actually enjoy the emotional experience we call worrying so how, by any stretch of the imagination, can it be described as psychologically comfortable? Well, the answer is it is only *relatively* comfortable. Many people delude themselves into thinking that worrying is the same as caring, and that it helps them to solve the problem. Unfortunately this is purely illusionary because, rather like a rabbit caught in headlights, worrying is more likely to immobilize you rather than stimulate you into appropriate action.

So, on balance, I think I must criticize the approach of keeping it to yourself and worrying about it. Actions solve problems and actions minus worry are more likely to be effective than worry plus actions or worry on its own. In short, worrying is superfluous and irrelevant to solving personal problems.

Grin and bear it

Grinning and bearing is certainly preferable to worrying, but this approach still has the major disadvantage of inactivity. At least it has the advantage of being outwardly cheerful but, in reality, it is a sort of stoic defeatism. Your energy is invested in fortitude rather than being directed at solving the problem. Maintaining uncrackable fortitude in the face of adversity is often hailed as praiseworthy, particularly by the stiff upper lip brigade. Men, in particular, have often been trained to believe that it is manly to grin and bear it, especially when it hurts. This can give them additional difficulties when it comes to owning up to personal problems. This partly explains why women spend more time

16

1. —
2. A
3. —
4. —
5. A
6. A
7. A
8. A
9. A
10. B

11/ B.

12/ A.

13/ —

14/ —

15/ B.

16/ A.

17/ A.

18/ B.

19/ A.

20/ —

21. A.
22. A.
23. A.
24. A.
25. —
26. A.
27. A.
28. B.
29. A.
30. A.

talking, writing and reading about personal problems. They are less handicapped than men at admitting to them in the first place. All things considered, it is also likely that women experience more personal problems than men. Sexual discrimination, even in advanced 'western' countries, is still rife and women tend to suffer more indignities on a daily basis than men do. The women's liberation movement is evidence that some women are disenchanted with grinning and bearing it. Perhaps, in a century or so's time, men will follow their lead!

Meanwhile, men have relationship and emotional problems too and, when the conditions are right and they feel 'safe' they'll readily admit to them. I've run an interpersonal skills programme for many years which concludes with a half-day problem-solving exercise. The participants (senior managers, and therefore usually men) are invited to describe a current relationship problem to a colleague on the course. The idea is to encourage them to talk about their problem to an uninvolved stranger and see if, together, they can arrive at a workable solution. In fifteen years' worth of experience, the number of people who claimed they had no personal problems can be counted on the fingers of one hand.

Everyone, senior or junior, rich or poor, intelligent or slow, has personal problems. The challenge is to create the conditions where the ignoring, discounting, worrying, and grinning stop and the admitting begins.

Grinning and bearing it is *not* a way to approach personal problems.

Grumble about it

Complaining about the people who, apparently, 'cause' our personal problems is almost a worldwide national pastime. As a professional collector of 'people-problems' it never fails to astonish me how prolific grumblers are. Sometimes people grumble without any prodding at all. At other times they need the encouragement of a few sympathetic 'ums and ahs' and then they start.

Certainly, as a psychologist keen to make people 'open up' about personal problems, I've never found that it required much skill on my part!

You can either grumble *to* someone or *about* someone. If you grumble behind people's backs, to an uninvolved party, it is an excellent way to win sympathy and attention. There is a good chance that your listener will bolster you by telling you you're right, and confirming that you're the injured victim. 'Oh! I don't know how you stand it.' This, of course, does wonders for your morale but little else to solve the problem. If you select your listener wisely he may realize that grumbling is achieving little and coax you into thinking of positive courses of action. When I'm counselling people with problems I use a simple, but effective, technique to bring the grumbling to a halt. I make them pretend that they have a magic wand and grant them three wishes. Apart from wishing that the people causing the problem would vanish they are allowed to wish anything – the more fanciful the better. This dramatically switches them from grumbling to having ideas and we go on from there to find a solution.

If you grumble to the involved person you can at least expect to gain their attention – even if it's negative and temporary.

So, grumbling certainly has its plus points. The trouble with it is that it is inadequate in making any lasting impact on entrenched personal problems at the thick end of the wedge. Grumbling *can* work with the occasional problem such as returning faulty goods to a shop, or complaining about poor service in a restaurant. It doesn't succeed so well with the sort of personal problems we are concerned with because, rather like 'crying wolf' too often, grumbling loses its short, sharp effect if it becomes persistent. Grumbling also puts the burden for making changes on to the other person and, after being on the receiving end of incessant grumbling, it is likely that the person will become aggrieved. As we shall see, there is a great deal more to solving personal problems than merely grumbling about them.

Talk it over with a friend

The saying goes 'a problem shared is a problem halved'. There is no doubt that talking to *anyone*, friend or stranger, has a useful therapeutic effect. You feel better as a result, even though the circumstances of the problem remain unchanged.

You might think twice before sharing confidences with a friend, fearing indiscretions. Your personal problem is more likely to be newsworthy to a friend than to a complete stranger. If they are part of a network of friends and acquaintances it may be unreasonable to expect them to remain completely quiet about it.

A friend is, by definition, an interested, if not involved party. Apart from the risk of gossip, it is unlikely that they are unbiased – they may even have an axe of their own to grind. Friends are, therefore, likely to 'take sides' and offer one-sided advice. This may be exactly what you want of course, since *your* friend is likely to side with *you*, but it may impair the quality of any advice offered. Generally speaking, the more unbiased and dispassionate the advice the better. Friends are not necessarily the best equipped to offer this.

Another potential snag with talking things over with a friend is that the friend may be a poor listener. The therapeutic effect of 'getting things off your chest' is considerably lessened if your friend won't let you get a word in edgeways! Your initial admission to a personal problem may trigger a whole host of reciprocal admissions and anecdotes. You are in danger of being left with your original problem *plus* one or two extra ones of theirs! While this is hardly the outcome you had in mind, it can still help you to put your own problem in perspective.

The crucial point, if you are going to talk over a problem with a friend, is to be clear what you want your friend to do for you. Do you merely want a shoulder to cry on? Or do you want them to give you advice? Or do you want them to help you work out a solution? These are three quite different roles. The first requires them to listen and be sympathetic. The second requires them to

19

suggest ideas. The third requires them to tease ideas out of you. If you are clear which role you want your friend to adopt, you are more likely to be able to convey this to them and less likely to be disappointed.

Talk it over with a stranger

An obvious way of avoiding the snags involved in sharing your problem with a friend is to talk it over with someone who is completely uninvolved and disinterested. This option retains all the therapeutic benefits associated with admitting to a problem and, depending on the stranger, offers other advantages as well.

Clearly, a stranger to you and your problem has to start from scratch, whereas a friend already has a great deal of prior knowledge to draw on. At first sight this may appear to be a minus point for strangers and a plus point for friends. In my experience it is, however, the other way round. The fact that a stranger starts from a position of no prior knowledge *forces* them to do useful but basic things such as asking questions and listening to your answers. A friend, on the other hand, is more likely to make assumptions and jump to conclusions. Furthermore, a stranger is better able to see the problem objectively and therefore more likely to come up with a fresh approach to it. It's surprising how often a stranger can suggest something that strikes you as both interesting and novel. They are better equipped to do this than friends because they are not overburdened with all the different sides of the situation. The less they know, the less likely they are to get bogged down.

A potential snag with the option of talking your problem over with a stranger is where to locate a suitable one. Friends are certainly handier! There are voluntary organizations who are in business to provide properly trained 'strangers' at any time of the day or night. The Samaritans come to mind immediately, and there are plenty more who have emulated them by offering emergency contact points. The very fact that you have to take positive action to search out a stranger makes it more likely that you will have made a conscious decision to use this option rather than blurting out your problem to a friend on the spur of the moment. You will probably have clearer expectations and be more purposeful and businesslike with a stranger than with a friend.

Yet another potential advantage with this option is that there is no danger of longer-term embarrassment or awkwardness. Friends you see again; strangers, like passing ships, you need never see again.

All in all, I am convinced that talking over your personal problem with a stranger is a more fruitful approach than using a friend. It's clearly harder to organize – but even that has its advantages.

Seek professional advice

There are a whole host of professionals you could take your problems to; clergymen, counsellors, doctors, therapists, psychiatrists, psychoanalysts, problem page 'aunties', and many more. Even with professionals a lot still depends on the skill of the individual – just as we have seen with friends and strangers.

Some professionals are notorious for offering ready-made 'packages' of advice. This is because professionals tend to specialize in certain *types* of problems and they are more or less obliged to make your problem fit with their special field. A classic example of this is depression. If you go to a cleryman he'll encourage your faith, if you go to your GP he'll prescribe pills or tell you to pull yourself together, if you go to an analyst he may trace your problem back to your childhood. There are, of course, exceptions. Some clergy have been trained in counselling skills, some doctors treat the whole person rather than an illness in isolation, some therapists concern themselves with the present, rather than delving back into the past. Generally speaking, however, professionals give best value when dealing with specific, defined problems rather than generalized or undefined ones with a mixture of interrelated factors. This is precisely why there are more acknowledged experts with medical and legal problems than with deep-rooted psychological ones.

Professional advice can cost money. Friends and voluntary 'strangers' are certainly cheaper. If you don't pay for the advice (or at least not directly), then professionals can be in such demand that you have to wait for an appointment and, when you get one, you may be spared only ten minutes or so in their presence. Psychological problems cannot be adequately diagnosed, and certainly cannot be solved, in ten minutes. An hour is more realistic. Marriage guidance counsellors, for example, allocate an hour for each session. Counselling sessions can be spread over many weeks, giving a total of ten or more hours of professional attention (marriage guidance counsellors are professional by virtue of their selection and training, even though they operate as volunteers on a part-time basis).

Another possible snag with professionals is that they tend to proffer advice rather than helping you seek out a useful solution. Professionals, even though they may disclaim it, are widely regarded as 'experts' and experts are expected to have the answers. Answers from the expert have a nasty habit of not being applicable in your particular case. The best professionals realize that when they give advice it will only be accepted if it confirms what you already had in mind. So, consulting an expert can be useful if only as final confirmation that what you have decided to do makes sense.

Guidelines for seeking out appropriate professional advice are similar to the ones we discussed in the last section, on strangers. Be clear what you want, in particular whether it is confirmatory advice or more general guidance/counselling. Be able to describe your problem clearly (professionals call this your 'presenting problem' because they try to dig deeper and uncover the real problem), and be prepared to wait for an appointment and/or pay for the professional's time (even voluntary counselling services recommend contributions in the form of fees that they waive in cases of real financial hardship).

Become better informed

There are many ways to become better informed about your personal problems. There are hundreds of books and articles. There are societies and self-help groups for everything imaginable. In fact, your biggest problem may be how to be selective about the vast amounts of available information.

With books, the most sensible policy is to start with one and forget about all the others. You can't read six books at the same time. The one you choose should always have suggestions for further reading. This makes it easier to continue your reading because one book leads you to another, and so on, for as long as you wish to pursue the subject.

An excellent way to become better informed is to join a self-help group of people with similar problems. This may take some initial courage since it means to admitting your problem to strangers, en masse! If you can locate a local group it's definitely worth a try, because groups that are bound together by a common interest are well equipped to provide mutual support. Swopping experiences with like-minded people is both therapeutic and can often give you fresh leads and ideas. The larger, established groups are often affiliated to a regional, or national, network and they are then likely to be an excellent source of up-to-date information. Clearly, a well organized established group can call on a greater range of resources and indulge in a wider spread of activities. They may have their own library, they may bring in outside speakers, they may have adopted their own professional advisers, they may even commission research projects and conduct surveys of their own.

If there isn't a suitable group in your area then that's no excuse! Go ahead and form one. It's easy. A year or so ago a young friend of ours was abandoned by her husband, leaving her with a three-year-old toddler. After a few months of loneliness and listlessness, she decided to make contact with a local 'singles' group. She went to a couple of meetings, and found that she had little in common with the other members. So she put a carefully worded advertisement in the local paper, and now runs a small group for divorced mothers with young children. Besides providing emotional support, they have their own baby-sitting service, they go on picnics together with all the children, and throw the occasional party. Whatever your problem, it's bound to be shared by a number of people in your area. Locating them by, for example, putting an advertisement in your local paper is simpler than you think.

Mutually supportive groups are very helpful. They are a good focal point for relevant information, either from books or from people with similar problems.

Talk it over with God

Talking your problem over with God is a great deal easier than talking it over with a human being. There is no risk of rebuttal, or embarrassment, or that He will hog the conversation. He doesn't ask any questions, He doesn't give specific or too obvious advice.

He didn't always behave like this, however. If we assume, for a moment, that the Bible is an authentic account of God's behaviour, we'll see that He has changed his style quite dramatically. Initially He adopted an extremely autocratic style. Examples? His wrath with Adam and Eve, 'cursed is the ground because of you'. The flood, 'I will wipe mankind, whom I have created, from the face of the earth'. Then he put trust in selected individuals such as Abraham ('I will surely bless you . . . because you have obeyed me'); Moses ('I will help you speak and will teach you what to say') and Isaiah ('Here is my servant whom I uphold, My chosen one in whom I delight'). Gradually His dealings with human beings became less directive. He sent His only son but revealed it to a mere handful of people and, when Jesus did declare himself, he spoke mainly in parables that were open to differing interpretations.

Despite, or because of, the fact that God does not direct you in a defined way, talking problems over with Him has the 'getting-it-off-your-chest' therapeutic effect, besides clarifying your mind

24

about all the different sides of the problem. If you go into a church to do your praying you have the added benefits of cool, peaceful, and beautiful surroundings.

So, if you believe in a caring God He is always worth a try. The chances are that He won't intervene to solve your problem for you but the process of talking things over with Him can help you decide what to do. Even if you don't believe in God, the relaxing effect of thinking things over in a quiet church can help. It's a low risk and an inexpensive approach. I'm reminded of a poster I saw outside a chapel recently. In large letters it said, 'If you can't stand life's problems – try kneeling!'.

Be honest with the person causing the problem

It's amazing how often this approach has been overlooked, or considered and rejected. Often I interrupt the flow of incessant grumbling to inquire 'Have you told them you feel like this?'. Invariably the answer is 'Well no, I didn't think it would help', or even 'It sounds daft, but I never even thought of it'.

Being honest with the person who is causing the problem is *always* worth a try. At worst it clears the air, at best it might do the trick and jolt them into changing their behaviour. It is important, however, to be realistic. Personal problems that have built up over a period of time take time to solve. You should consider yourself lucky if honesty causes them to make the desired adjustments. There is, usually, more to solving personal problems than that.

Being open involves telling the person quite candidly that something they do is causing you a problem. How you do this is crucial. It should be done in a way that doesn't sound accusing or critical. If they think they are being attacked they'll rush to their own defence or even go on the offensive and criticize you! It helps to get this right if you remember that you are the person with the problems – not them. Pretend it's *your* fault so that you do not seem to be accusing them.

Being honest works best when the person concerned is

25

'mature', in the sense that they welcome hearing about the effect their behaviour has on other people. You may retort that, in your experience, mature people are few and far between – non-existent even. But people are generally interested in what others think of them, and, if you are honest and uncritical you will often succeed in winning their constructive attention.

It also helps considerably if you are telling them something that they did not realize. When they are genuinely oblivious to the fact that they were causing you a problem, your information is often enough to guarantee their interest. If they have heard it all before, it is more likely to be perceived, by them, as grumbling or nagging.

Timing is also important. You are more likely to be able to discuss the problem in a dispassionate, uncritical way if you do it at a time when the behaviour is absent. If you do it when you are feeling aggrieved about the latest manifestation of the problem you are more likely to become angry and start criticizing. This advice runs counter to common sense which would indicate that it is best to approach the person at the time the problem behaviour occurs. I advocate on-the-spot discussion if the problem is still in its early stages – at the thin end of the wedge, but if it has become entrenched then any discussion may develop into a heated argument.

Sometimes people are afraid that being honest will actually make matters worse. I concede that there are some hard, immature cases where honesty provokes an explosive response. But, if you choose your person, your topic and your time, you at least minimize the chances of it backfiring on you. In the majority of cases revealing the problem to the person concerned, done properly, is worth a try.

Persuade the problem person to change

Many of the things we've said about honest discussion also apply to persuasion. The difference is that persuasion goes further than merely giving the problem person information. When you attempt to persuade someone, you are actively urging them to do something – in the case of personal problems, to change something.

Persuasion is an obvious thing to try. Success depends on getting the person to see reason and the benefits (to them, not just to you), of making a change. If you manage that you will have succeeded in winning intellectual consent. This still leaves the vital business of getting them to tackle the upheaval involved in actually changing. To do this, they need to see exactly what they have to do to effect the required change. Beyond that, they need constant support and encouragement while they make the necessary modifications. So there is more to successful persuasion than meets the eye. Not surprisingly, most people underestimate what is involved in persuading someone to change. Winning verbal agreement, or intellectual assent, is only half the story. It is getting someone to *do* something that counts. This is why the benefits to them and the specific action steps are such vital ingredients. The world is littered with disappointed people who thought, at the end of the conversation, they had been successful in persuading someone, only to discover later that they hadn't.

If you accept that actual change is the measure of successful persuasion, perhaps you can begin to see why it has its limitations in the case of entrenched personal problems. The main problem is that persuasion, while it goes further than being honest, stops short of giving sufficient assistance to the person who is causing the problem. It leaves them with the considerable difficulty of making a change. If we take, as an example, persuading someone to give up smoking, or to reduce their intake of saturated fats. The magnitude of the struggle involved in making changes such as these varies from person to person but, for most, it amounts to very much more than 'knowing it makes sense'. In spite of persuasion to the contrary people will still persist in resisting change, wasting energy, smoking, drinking, eating too much of the wrong foods, not taking enough exercise, rioting, and vandalizing.

Of course, persuasion often succeeds in bringing about

27

temporary change. 'Giving up smoking is easy, I've done it loads of times.' This happens when the benefits of returning to the old behaviour, smoking for example, outweigh the benefits of sticking to the new behaviour, not smoking. It serves to underline the importance of supporting people right through the period of change rather than leaving them to do it alone.

Even though persuasion doesn't always produce impressive results, I certainly think it is worth trying, but don't be disappointed if it doesn't bring about permanent change.

Conclusion

We have looked briefly at a dozen different approaches. No doubt you can think of more. We haven't, for example, discussed getting a third party to liaise or arbitrate on your behalf. Neither have we examined the option of forcing someone to change by bringing various pressures to bear on them. In Chapter 4 we shall look at another method of solving personal problems – an approach that often works when all else has failed.

3

Some Myths Exposed

In the last chapter we saw that people often find it difficult to admit, either to themselves or to someone else, their personal problems. This is largely because of the tendency to seek psychological comfort by conveniently ignoring or distorting reality. Even after a problem has been admitted, we saw that there were hazards in choosing an appropriate approach. Under pressure from the circumstances of the problem it is all too tempting to take the line of least resistance. Unfortunately, the easiest and most obvious approach is unlikely to be adequate in giving a permanent solution to the problem. This is because the easiest approach is selected more with an eye on what is convenient *to us* than on what is suitable *for the problem*.

Personal problems, just like any other problems, have to be faced up to, realistically analysed and a feasible solution carefully planned and put into action. Unfortunately, we rarely manage to tackle our personal problems in such a clear-headed way. In fact, we are much more likely to be systematic when we have problems with things as opposed to people. If a machine gives us a problem we are more likely to investigate it, searching for the cause, eliminate certain possibilities and, if need be, enlist appropriate aid to fix the problem. Such rational, systematic approaches are just as helpful with personal problems.

This chapter will show why we find it so difficult to be clear and objective about our personal problems. In it we will expose a number of fictitious beliefs that tend to handicap the way we approach personal problems.

Myth 1: That someone, somewhere, has the perfect answer and will tell you exactly what to do and take full responsibility for the outcome

What a delightful illusion! Your only problem is to track down

The Person. My guess is that you'll never find him, or her, simply because they don't exist. While you are searching, in vain, for the pot of gold at the end of the rainbow, you could be solving your personal problems.

In fact, this isn't one myth, it's four.

First, it holds out hope that someone else will take over *your* problem. Unfortunately this is impossible. If it's *your* problem it stays your problem. No one can take it away from you however much you wish they would. Other people can certainly help you with your problem – but it remains yours. You are the problem-owner.

Secondly, it presupposes that there is a perfect answer. This is most unlikely and certainly not worth fretting over. It is not perfection we are after, merely a feasible, practical solution! If we become neurotic about finding the perfect answer it will inevitably delay us in making a less than perfect solution. Answers to personal problems do not come hand-carved on tablets of stone.

Thirdly, it anticipates that you will be told exactly what to do. Even if you were told you would, probably, resent it. Most people react badly to autocratic instructions, unless they come from someone held in high esteem. The chances are that advice is the best you will get. Then it is up to you to decide what to do.

Finally, this myth suggests that you will not be held responsible for the outcome. This is the 'I was only obeying orders' syndrome. Even if an 'expert' told you what to do, you would remain responsible for your actions. Like it or not, we are *always* accountable for our own actions.

Myth 2: That personal problems can be solved 'at a stroke'

On rare occasions we might be lucky, but it is safer to expect personal problems to take some time to shift. As we saw in the last chapter, being honest with the problem person or persuading them to change can sometimes do the trick. Usually, however, problems have taken time to progress to the thick end of the wedge and will, therefore, need time (not, fortunately, anything like as long) to unravel. In later chapters we will see how this applies to personal problems, but meanwhile a sporting analogy may help to illustrate the point. Imagine you are an accomplished tennis player but that gradually a fault creeps into your serve. At first the fault is imperceptible, but eventually it becomes apparent that you've slipped into the habit of taking your eye off the ball at the crucial moment. Having identified the problem (and that might have taken some doing), you then, in effect, have to 'unlearn' the bad habit and replace it with a good habit. Forgive the pun, but this couldn't be done 'at a stroke'. It would require practice. The analogy extends to personal problems. They too take time to develop and the people involved need time to unlearn and relearn their actions.

Myth 3: That there isn't any solution

Sometimes personal problems seem so complex and difficult that we despair of finding any solution, perfect or imperfect. This happens when the gap between what we've got and what we want is overwhelmingly large. Clearly things can seem pretty grim, and there are plenty of superstitions about fate, bad luck (seven years for breaking a mirror), and accidents happening in threes.

Grave though the problems might be I always maintain there are many potential solutions. A potential solution spells out something that you *could* do, even though you might not *want* to. The reason why so many problems seem insoluble is because we muddle up our 'coulds' and 'wants'. Faced with a problem there are many options – things we could do. Each is a potential solution. It may be that we baulk at implementing all of them but that doesn't alter the fact that there are solutions, merely that the solutions are, for one reason or another, unacceptable to us.

Admittedly, what we really want are solutions that work. A workable solution is a course of action that you both can, and want, to put into action. Any good problem-solving approach will have to meet both these requirements. The technique I introduce in the next chapter, and examine in various ways for the remainder of the book, generates potential solutions (coulds), and then goes on to whittle them down into workable solutions (wants). Distinguishing 'coulds' from 'wants' helps us to be more optimisitic about the possibility of solving any personal problem.

The sheer complexity of many pesonal problems is another reason why we are often overwhelmed. The difficulty is knowing where to start. Once we have established an initial foothold, however tenuous, the way ahead seems easier. Often the secret of success is to break a large problem down into smaller bits, and decide which bit to make a start on. This works with many big undertakings (and tackling personal problems is a big undertaking). If, for example, I sat down to write this book, armed with 300 sheets of blank writing paper, ten biros and a dictionary, it's unlikely that I would ever complete it. The task seen as a whole is too daunting. The few pages I produced the first day would seem utterly insignificant. If, however, I break the overall task down into a series of chapters, and chapters down into sections, then I can set myself day by day, attainable mini-targets, get the job done and feel a sense of achievement at each stage.

So problems, particularly the big, complex, entrenched, personal problems, need to be broken down into mini-problems. The *objective* is to solve the big problem, the *plan* is to tackle it in manageable stages. Knowing how to do this helps us to be optimistic about solving any problem, however daunting.

Myth 4: That problems are punishments from God

If you believe that problems are punishments for past misdemeanours, then you are likely to accept problems passively rather than tackle them positively. Obviously punishments, especially from God, are not to be taken lightly. If it is just (and surely it would be if God had administered it), and the punishment fits the crime then who are we to do anything to alleviate it?

I can't of course prove it, but it seems to me most unlikely that God gives personal problems as punishments. If you believe that God has a hand in your problems then it makes much more sense to see them as His way of testing you. We are supposed to be subservient and repentant when punished but challenged and stimulated when tested. Surely God wants to do His best to develop us, rather than bash us into submission? I argued in the last chapter that God seems to have modified the rather short-tempered approach He initially used in His dealings with us. He has replaced it with a much more thoughtful, patient style. I'm sure that God, if He exists and if He cares, is primarily interested in how we solve our problems and disappointed when we succumb to defeatism. He is interested in our success, not in our failure.

Myth 5: That doing something will only make matters worse

Often personal problems are so delicately poised, like a house of cards, that you feel even the slightest movement will bring about a catastrophe. Nothing must be done to disturb the familiarity of the current equilibrium. Better the devil you know . . . and all that.

This harks back to the business of risk that we were discussing at the beginning of the last chapter. As we saw then, fear of the unknown is a major excuse for doing nothing. An even greater inhibition is the dread that taking action will actually make matters worse.

To be honest, this is an inevitable part of the risk involved in doing something in a bid to solve the problem. The risk is increased, however, if we plunge headlong into taking action on a purely spontaneous basis. The risk is greatly reduced if we consider carefully the pros and cons of the action we have in mind, before we take it. Formal decision-making techniques, used in industry, encourage the decision maker to list as many alternative actions as possible, and to assess the relative risks of each, by giving them a numerical weighting. The decision maker is also invited to anticipate the worst that could go wrong with each action, before finally coming to a considered decision about the best course of action. We need to adopt the same kind of safeguards against the hazards of taking ill-considered action.

Ironically, the more emotive the problem we are faced with,

the more likely we are to be panicked into taking some piece of hasty action. The actions we take under duress are the sort we invariably regret later, in the cool light of day.

Much better to have a rational problem-solving technique to cling to that will increase the probability of doing something to make matters better, not worse. Just such a technique will be introduced in the next chapter.

Myth 6: That it would be lovely to have no problems

No it wouldn't! It would be boring. No need to worry though because running out of personal problems is definitely not a possibility! Satisfaction with what we've got (in other words, no problems) is always shortlived. It is rather like climbing an endless mountain with a series of peaks, each one appearing to be the final summit. As we reach one peak we see the next, and set our sights on that.

I can remember being totally convinced that when I earned enough money to get a mortgage on a house I would be satisfied. And so I was – for about a week. Then the aim was to extend the garage to take a deep freeze. That achieved, I wanted a bigger garden, colour television, a new car. Eventually I broke through the materialistic barrier. Now I wanted people to recognize me as a competent professional. Then as a caring member of society (so I flung myself into charity work of various kinds). And now, further up the hierarchy, my problems are far more challenging than they have ever been. Where do I stand? What are my fundamental beliefs? What shall I spend my time doing? Do I like myself? Am I learning from experience or just becoming more pigheaded? What's it all about anyway? My father-in-law, a retired clergyman, once told me that he always thought he would become more certain, even wiser, as he grew older. Instead he confessed that he had become less certain about everything. Perhaps that's what wisdom is all about – fewer answers and more problems.

Myth 7: That it's all their fault

They say it takes two to argue, but it only takes one to create a personal problem, and that one is *you*.

This may seem hard to accept but, as we explore personal problems in more depth, I hope to convince you that, in the majority of cases, you, intentionally or unintentionally, *create* your problems. By definition, personal problems belong to you and your actions and reactions are always the most vital ingredient. Of course, it is very convenient to blame other people for our problems; we are whiter than white, it's all their fault. Unfortunately I've never yet come across a single case where this was true. Even when it seemed obvious the problem stemmed solely from someone else's unprovoked actions, closer examination revealed that their actions were reactions to someone else's actions (if you see what I mean!).

Let's take an example. Suppose I complain to you that my wife keeps nagging me. It's highly likely that I will make it sound as if it is all her fault. She has this unfortunate behaviour pattern; I am the innocent victim. If you probed further, however, you would establish that my wife's behaviour varies. She doesn't *always* nag, sometimes she praises, at other times she discusses, or she may laugh and so on. So the question becomes, when does she nag? What happens to stimulate this particular behaviour? The answer is she nags when:

I haven't kept up with routine maintenance chores about the house (things like taps dripping, pelmets that need rawplugging, windows that stick, etc.)

I come bowling in, full of the joys of spring, enthusing about the stimulating day I've had.

I don't bother to inquire about her day and/or listen when she tells me about it.

So, you see, unwittingly I created the problem. It is not all my wife's fault, even though initially I may have thought it was.

On closer analysis, all relationship problems between people are like this. Our actions, not just theirs, are part of the picture.

This means we need to point the finger at ourselves, rather than at other people.

This may strike you as a rather depressing revelation. In practice, however, it gives us the key to solving personal problems. If our actions stimulate other people's actions then we ought to be able to alter other people's actions by altering ourselves. The focus is on us, not on them.

Myth 8: That people are unpredictable

You often hear people saying 'You never know what she's going to do next' and, 'He always keeps us guessing', but people are a great deal more predictable than our weather!

People are certainly complex and, like the weather, the rules governing their behaviour are not completely understood as yet. While research continues to put together the jigsaw puzzle, we have to do our best to understand what makes people 'tick'.

It all becomes clearer if you start with people's actions, rather than their personality as a whole. Think of someone you know really well. Your partner, your child, your best friend perhaps. Can you anticipate, with any degree of accuracy, how they would react if you stuck a pin into them? What if you hid behind a door and leapt out on them with a loud 'boo'? The chances are you can predict their reactions with some certainty. Now let's think about some more difficult examples. Suppose you asked them the time or the date, would they answer you? How would they react if you flatly disagreed with something they had just said? What about their reaction if you crack a joke they haven't heard before?

Assuming you know the person well, in other words, that you have sampled the way they tend to behave in a variety of different situations, you can probably predict their reactions to various happenings reasonably accurately. So, people, once you get to know them, are predictable.

Even if you don't know them you can have a pretty good stab at anticipating their reactions. For the last ten years I have been investigating to see if it is possible to predict reactions to certain communication behaviours. The results show that it is. For example, if you disagree with someone there is a 42 per cent probability that they will become defensive and enlarge on their idea. If you ask someone for their ideas about how to solve a problem there is a 79 per cent probability they will put forward an idea, however tentative. If you ask someone to clarify a question there is an 89 per cent probability they will provide the clarification you want.

Predictions of this magnitude, while never indicating things are 100 per cent certain, certainly demonstrate that people's behaviour is astonishingly predictable. I once sat in as an observer at a tricky management meeting. There were many sensitive issues on the agenda. The senior manager, chairing the meeting, was obviously tense and edgy. At intervals he grabbed a pencil and thrust it into the jaws of an electric pencil sharpener. After this had happened three or four times I noticed that it was an early warning, signifying that he was about to lose his temper. It was uncannily predictable, yet no one else in the meeting linked the two events. It isn't that people are unpredictable, merely that all too often we are not observant enough to read the signs.

Myth 9: That people don't/can't change

'You can't teach an old dog new tricks', 'A leopard doesn't change his spots', 'Human nature doesn't change' – pessimism abounds.

Apparently the evidence is stacked against people changing. I myself have just been arguing that people are largely predictable so, surely, it would now be contradictory to turn round and say they change? It is certainly true that, as you reflect on the people you know, you can probably see strong threads of consistency running through their behaviour. Rather like a stick of rock with the resort's name through the middle, people's actions have the stamp of their personality running through them.

Accepting, for a moment, that people generally stick to tried and trusted ways of behaving with very little deviation, the question we have to ask is this: is this inevitable, or is it possible for people to change? This question is crucial in the context of personal problems. If, in the nature of things, no one can change, it is obviously hopeless to attempt to solve personal problems.

The issue of whether people *can* change becomes clearer if we consider for a moment what constitutes a change. Are we thinking of dramatic 'U' turns, or lesser right-angled turns, or just small deflections a few degrees either side of the general course of direction? Total personality changes, though rare, are possible, usually as a result of traumatic events such as brain damage or a serious illness. Fortunately we don't need to make dramatic, 180 degree changes to other people, or ourselves, in order to solve personal problems. Lesser modifications are all that we require. We want someone to ask once, instead of nagging. We want someone to criticize constructively rather than destructively. We want someone to say less and listen more.

These are realistic modifications or changes.

How do you decide whether a change is realistic? The vital thing is to consider whether the person is *capable* of doing whatever it is you want them to do. A novel way to do this is to say to yourself, 'Is this something they could not do, even under hypnosis?' This is an interesting way of thinking about what changes are possible, because people under hypnosis are more open to suggestion and less resistant to change than at any other time. I'm not suggesting, for a moment, that you need to hypnotize people in order to change them, merely that if you use this as a check, it will help you to be realistic about how many changes are possible.

The reason why people don't change as often as they could is because the circumstances surrounding their behaviour either remain much the same or seem to them to be so similar that change is not required. If nothing changes around them people very sensibly carry on behaving the way they have learned to. The key to changing people's behaviour, therefore, is to make changes to their environment so that their characteristic ways of behaving are no longer appropriate. People both can, and do, change when it suits them to do so.

Myth 10: That people's actions are caused by underlying personality traits

If you believe this – and most people do – it seriously complicates the business of solving problems with people. In fact, you must be very cynical about the possibility of being able to solve them at all.

We all know that if you want to solve a problem properly you must tackle its root causes rather than tinkering about with symptoms. If you believe that the root causes of people's actions lie somewhere deep within their personality then it follows that you will need to delve down to identify the real causes and do something to change them.

Let's illustrate this by returning to the example of my nagging wife. If we assume her nagging is an outward symptom with deeper underlying causes, we need to identify and change them. In our quest to track down the real causes we might think about her motives, attitudes, and feelings. She might be nagging me because she wants (motive) to bring me down a peg or two. On the other hand she might be nagging me because she is depressed (feeling), or because she believes (attitude) it isn't fair for me to go out enjoying myself while she is stuck at home, surrounded by dripping taps.

Now let's suppose, for the sake of argument, that these *are* underlying causes of her nagging behaviour. Two questions. First, what do you suggest I do to change them? Secondly, if I changed them *and nothing else*, would you be confident that the nagging would disappear? If you are honest, your answer to both questions should be 'I'm not sure'.

Nobody knows what to do to change someone's motives, attitudes, or feelings in the required direction. It is an awfully hit and miss affair. You can argue with people till you are blue in the face, bombard them with propaganda, try to persuade them, threaten them, even bribe them but the fact remains that they, and they alone, control their motives, attitudes, and feelings. It is exactly like leading a horse to water but not being able to force it to drink.

Suppose, however, I was fortunate and succeeded in influencing my wife's motives, attitudes, or feelings. Would the removal of these internal 'causes' have the required effect to her outward behaviour? I'd say no, because we have done nothing to alter the external circumstances that provoke the nagging. If I continue to neglect my maintenance chores, enthuse about my stimulating day and fail to inquire about her day, it is predictable that she will nag. These external happenings are as much causes of the nagging as the internal personality factors are.

Our assumption that the nagging was caused by underlying things like motives, attitudes, and feelings meant that we ignored the more straightforward causes of the nagging. People's actions always have external, as well as internal, causes. What's more, it is far easier to change the obvious, external causes than to grope around wrestling with intangible things like motives, attitudes, and feelings.

To sum up: people's actions are not exclusively caused by underlying personality traits. They are only half the story. The external causes are equally important and when it comes to solving personal problems, we shall see they are more significant.

4

How to Solve Personal Problems

The time has come to reveal another approach to solving personal problems. In this chapter I will introduce the method, and demonstrate how it works, by using two short case studies. In subsequent chapters the approach will be examined more carefully and Chapter 6 gives many more examples of how it works in practice.

Let's start with a couple of case studies.

The case of the chauvinistic husband

Susan has been married to Ed for twelve years. They have three children ranged at eighteen-month intervals, the youngest being nearly eight years old. Ed runs his own business, as a small jobbing printer, but times are hard and money is tight. Susan did a secretarial course after leaving school and it was always understood that she'd take a job when the children were older and settled into school. When Ed's business began to decline Susan was only too happy to volunteer to find a job doing secretarial work. Two months ago she started work in a solicitor's office in the market town where they live. She would have preferred part-time work but secretarial jobs are scarce in the locality and so she grabbed the nine to five job gratefully.

After two months of tackling a full-time job *and* running the house, Susan is worn to a frazzle. She gets up early to do housework and to give everyone a good breakfast. She spends most lunchtimes shopping for essential stores. By four o'clock each afternoon she is watching the clock and worrying about the children coming home from school to an empty house. At five she rushes home to prepare an evening meal. After that she usually irons or mends, with half an eye on the television, and falls asleep as soon as her head hits the pillow.

During this period her relations with Ed have taken a turn for the worse. He comes home later than he used to each evening. He never troubles to inquire about her day, and comments if everything isn't 'just so' when he arrives home. When he lends a hand with household chores he does so with ill grace, and usually only after she has nagged him or lost her temper. Rows are on the increase, sex is on the decrease.

Susan feels that the only solution is to give up her job and, once again, devote her undivided attention to the home.

The case of the sexually harassed secretary

Joy works in a large open plan office where she is secretary to the data processing manager. Joy is a bright girl and a very competent secretary. She has always been self-conscious about her size. She is nearly six feet tall and has a big bust and bottom. All through school she was teased about her size (she developed earlier than most of her contemporaries), and has never had a boy friend.

At present Joy, twenty-three, lives at home with her parents, though she realizes she'll have to make the break soon. Meanwhile she is happy at home. She listens to her stereoplayer and is an avid reader – particularly of biographies and travel. She much prefers the peace of her own home because her life at work is dogged with persistent teasing and unpleasantness. Her boss is all right but some of the programmers in the office annoy her with their irritating remarks. If she says something innocent such as 'Do you want it this afternoon?' (referring to a piece of typing), as quick as a flash they'll retort 'Any time dear', or 'I never thought you'd ask'. Jokes about big 'boobs' and 'being a bit of a handful' are legion. Frequently she finds photographs cut out of girlie magazines underneath her typewriter cover. The other day she found one advertising an inflatable doll called Joy. Across the top was scrawled 'Who pumps you up then?' and 'Feeling deflated?'. On another occasion she found a photograph of an obese nude with the added caption 'Your secret's out'.

The constant bombardment of sexual remarks is making Joy depressed. She finds it hard not to show some reaction. She used to merely blush, but now she swears at them and has even fled to the toilet in tears. She hesitates to raise it with her manager because she feels so embarrassed. Her parents are sympathetic and urge her to stick it out – 'They'll soon get fed up'. But, as the months pass, Joy is alarmed to find that the remarks and the teasing persist.

If these problems are not particularly similar to yours then don't despair. They are only *examples* to illustrate how to solve personal problems successfully. It will not matter if none of the problems in this book corresponds closely to yours. Indeed, it would be surprising if they did, since we've already said that personal problems belong to individuals. Other people's personal problems will, inevitably, be mere anecdotes to you (and, it's worth remembering, vice versa!).

As you read the descriptions of the problems, you may have found yourself being unsympathetic with the two problem owners, Susan and Joy. It's all too easy to distance yourself and maintain that you would never have got yourself into such a mess. 'They should have had more sense', 'They should have seen it coming', 'She's no one but herself to blame'. And yet, it's worth remembering that these problems really happened (I've obviously changed the names to protect the innocent, but that's all), and that the people involved were genuinely troubled and perplexed. It's too easy to operate a double standard, regarding other people's personal problems as petty and only our own as substantial. Case study descriptions tend to aid and abet this tendency because the information presented in a case study has been tidied up, filtered and selected, whereas real-life problems are messy, unedited, and full of red herrings. This is why, in real life, it is difficult to see the wood for the trees. In a case study the problem, its causes, and potential solutions are a great deal easier to spot.

A different method of solving personal problems

If you have been reading 'between the lines' you should be able to guess some of the features of the problem-solving approach I am going to advise. The fact that I have already used the word behaviour many times, and been careful to distinguish it from underlying personality traits is a good clue. Another sure indicator of things to come is the emphasis on, not just behaviour, but also the external circumstances surrounding it.

The approach is an adapted, simplified version of Behaviour Modification or, as it is sometimes called, Behaviour Therapy. Unfortunately I'm only too aware that these sound alarmingly 'Big Brotherish'. Behaviour Modification, in its 120-year history, has been largely misunderstood and had a bad press more often than a good one. This is partly because Behaviour Modification techniques have not been presented as well as they might be but the main reason is undoubtedly that the method strikes people as unduly cold and calculating.

First impressions like these are entirely understandable (I can remember having exactly the same reservations when I first came across Behaviour Modification), but I intend to postpone discussion on all the objections until the approach has been introduced and demonstrated.

Despite its relative unpopularity, Behaviour Modification has an impressive record in helping people overcome many troublesome behaviour patterns. It has been used to break unwanted habits such as smoking, drinking, overeating, and stuttering. It has been successful in modifying violent behaviour and vandalism. But perhaps the most dramatic successes have been in helping people overcome fears and phobias of various kinds – fears of spiders, of flying, of the dark, of open spaces, of heights and so on. Behaviour Modification has also been used to help people overcome neurotic worries and stress, migraines, impotence, and high blood pressure.

Behaviour Modification has therefore proved itself by solving some substantial problems. If it has been so successful in tackling extreme disorders then you can be sure it will help in solving even the most obstinate personal problems that trouble and inconvenience us.

Let us now see how Behaviour Modification works by demonstrating its ability to solve the two personal problems described earlier. Since 'Behaviour Modification' is a bit of a mouthful, I shall refer to my version of it more simply as BMod. The BMod approach to solving personal problems has just three basic ingredients. Let us look at each in turn.

Behaviour

The most important ingredient in the BMod recipe is behaviour itself. You have probably been told to 'behave yourself' and 'be on your best behaviour' hundreds of times, if not recently then certainly when you were a child. This tends to give behaviour moralistic undertones as to whether it is good or bad, right or wrong, acceptable or unacceptable.

In BMod, however, we use the word behaviour in its 'pure' sense to refer to any overt, or obvious, action. Overt actions are plain to see and include everything we say to people as well as non-verbal movements such as facial expressions, gestures with hands and arms, and 'body language' in general. Behaviour is smiling, frowning, shaking someone's hand, giving someone 'two fingers', looking at someone when they are talking, doodling, agreeing, disagreeing, shouting, whispering, praising, criticizing – everything. Literally all you do and anyone else *does* is behaviour.

As its title suggests, behaviour is central to the BMod approach. The whole idea is to single out the behaviour that is causing the problem. This emphasis on behaviour is entirely appropriate because *all* the problems we have with other people result from the way they behave. It is their overt, plainly seen actions that give us the gap between what we want and what we've got. Look back at our case studies. In both the problem owner is plagued by someone else's *behaviour*. Susan is troubled by her husband's chauvinism. Joy is depressed by sexist remarks at the office. Of course we can speculate about the motives behind the behaviour and that may help us to become more tolerant, but it won't equip us to alter the behaviour that is causing the problem.

A major advantage of BMod is that its preoccupation with how people are actually behaving helps to make the problem clear. With personal problems in particular it is too easy to get bogged down in a morass of speculations about hidden, intangible factors. Personal problems that result from someone's behaviour can always be solved without getting swamped by the complexities of such things as motives, attitudes, or feelings. This is not to deny that these internal factors exist or to deny their undoubted influence on the way people behave. BMod merely claims that tackling behaviour directly is an easier, more straightforward way to solve personal problems than proceeding indirectly via underlying factors.

Triggers

A trigger is any event that happens *before* the behaviour in question. Any event can act as the trigger. It may be a spoken remark or just a 'meaningful' look. It may be a place, or a time of day, or a specific occurrence such as being caught in a traffic jam or being burgled. The BMod argument is that behaviour never happens in a vacuum. Something always triggers it in the same way that a chance incident, even a familiar smell, can trigger a memory. When solving personal problems, the trick is to single out from the mass of events the ones that are triggering the problem behaviour.

Let's see how this works with our two case study problems. Clearly Susan's problems with Ed have increased since she took a full-time job two months ago. This is the trigger for Ed's increased chauvinism. It is likely that he has always had chauvinistic tendencies, but his behaviour has undoubtedly worsened since Susan took her full-time job. In Joy's case the questions she asks with double meanings ('Do you want it this afternoon?') are triggers for sexist remarks at her expense. No doubt Joy's questions are perfectly innocent but they are sufficient to trigger the teasing behaviour of the male programmers.

Once we have succeeded in identifying the events that are triggering the behaviour in question we have a valuable foothold to solving the problem. If there is a link between such and such an event and the occurrence of the problem behaviour then we might be able to think of ways to break the link and therefore prevent the behaviour.

If, therefore, Susan's return to work is triggering an increase of chauvinistic behaviour from Ed then she could break the link by giving up her job. Similarly Joy could reduce sexist remarks at her expense by never asking any questions. Remove the trigger and you prevent the behaviour.

In practice, of course, things are not quite so staightforward. It would be absurd for Susan to surrender her job in order to prevent Ed's chauvinism. It would be impracticable for Joy to withhold all questions. I am not suggesting that these are necessarily *feasible* ways of solving these problems. At this stage I am merely demonstrating the link between triggers and behaviour and showing how changed triggers inevitably result in changed behaviour. In practice the object of the exercise is to find feasible, acceptable ways of modifying the events that trigger the behaviour. This refers back to the difference between what you could do and what you want to do that we mentioned in the last chapter. There are always plenty of things you could do to solve personal problems. Usually, all things considered, we have to strike a compromise and settle on a solution that we both can and want to put into action. More about how Susan and Joy did this to solve their problems after we have looked at the third ingredient in the BMod approach.

Effects

The final piece in the BMod jigsaw puzzle is by far the most important and explains why people persist in using certain behaviours in preference to others. Effects are anything that happens *after* the behaviour that are a satisfactory outcome *for the person*. Effects, like triggers, can be anything – other people's reactions, subsequent events, fame, money, literally anything providing it is regarded as 'nice' by the person who behaved.

After Ed has been chauvinistic (come home late, complained if things aren't 'just so', been ungracious about lending a hand) the effect on Susan is that she tries even harder to run the house as she used to before taking on a full-time job. This is an effect that suits Ed very well, thank you!

After the male programmers have made sexist remarks the effect on Joy is that she blushes and shows that she is upset. From the mickey-takers' point of view this is a splendid outcome. After all there wouldn't be much fun in teasing someone if it had no discernible effect.

Effects are a crucial ingredient in the BMod approach to solving personal problems because they throw light on why people behave as they do. Briefly the argument is this: without necessarily realizing it we all experiment, on a trial and error basis, with different ways of behaving. This experimentation starts almost as soon as we are born and continues unabated right through the so-called formative years, and beyond. Essentially what is happening is that we are learning, in a rough and ready fashion, which behaviours improve our circumstances and which behaviours don't. We then tend to repeat behaviours we consider a 'success' and abandon behaviours we consider a 'flop'.

We can see this clearly in babies just a few weeks old. From birth babies have the instinctive behaviour of crying. Because this is instinctive they don't have to learn to cry and initially they do it whenever they are uncomfortable. Triggers for crying are being slapped on the bottom, being hungry or thirsty, having a wet or soiled nappy on, etc. Quite quickly babies discover that when they cry nice things happen; someone comes and picks them up, feeds them, cuddles and strokes them and so on. Having made the discovery that crying has desirable effects (that 'nice' things happen after it) babies cry not just when they are uncomfortable but also when they want attention. I am not suggesting this learning process is conscious. It happens because babies, just like anyone else, connect certain behaviour with the effects it leads to.

Effects encourage people to repeat their behaviour even though it may create problems for someone else. Babies don't mind getting you up in the middle of the night as long as their crying results in a desirable effect. Any piece of behaviour that is successful in getting the right effects will be repeated regardless of the inconvenience to other people.

As we grow older we learn to achieve the effects we want rather more subtly. We learn to be polite, to give and take, co-operate, to get on with people and help them to achieve their effects rather than being determined to secure our own. Nevertheless it still remains true that people's behaviour results in effects.

As we shall see the effects are often obscure and difficult to identify but the BMod argument is that they are there, somewhere in the events that are churned up in the wake of a behaviour. In the last chapter I cited the example of my wife's nagging to illustrate how I unintentionally provoked this behaviour (by falling behind with routine maintenance in the house, by enthusing about my day without inquiring after hers, and so on). The examples I gave were all triggers and therefore only half the story. What were the effects, the events that happened *after* the nagging that were sufficiently 'nice' to cause my wife to adopt nagging as a useful behaviour? You can probably guess. Gradually over the years we have been married my wife discovered that I fixed things about the house a great deal faster after I had been nagged about them and postponed them indefinitely if I was not. From her point of view, the nagging worked. It was a successful behaviour and as such likely to be repeated again and again.

The BMod problem solving technique

Now that you have met the three BMod ingredients separately it is time to put them together and see how BMod works as a technique for solving problems resulting from other people's behaviour.

Just to recap, the BMod view is that no behaviour occurs in a vacuum. Something always happens before it and something always happens after it. These surrounding events are crucial because they explain why the person is behaving as they are and because they give us ideas on how we can solve the problem. Things that happen before the behaviour in question are called 'triggers'. Things that happen after the behaviour are called 'effects'.

While triggers and effects remain intact and linked to the behaviour it is predictable that the behaviour will continue. If either triggers or effects, or both, are changed then it is inevitable that the behaviour will change also. The way to solve problems caused by other people's behaviour is therefore as follows:

Step 1   Be clear and specific about the problem behaviour.

Step 2   Identify the events that trigger the behaviour.

Step 3   Identify the effects the behaviour results in.

Step 4   Be clear and specific about what behaviour you want (usually the opposite of the behaviour you have got).

Step 5   Work out how to change the triggers so that the problem behaviour is no longer triggered and the wanted behaviour is.

Step 6   Work out how to change the effects so that the problem behaviour is no longer encouraged and the wanted behaviour is.

Step 7   Check that your plan is feasible (that you really *can* put it into action and *want* to go through with it) and work out how to implement it (whether to tell the problem person what you are going to do, etc.).

Step 8   Finally, implement the changes and watch the problem behaviour decrease and the wanted behaviour increase.

Eight steps might strike you as rather daunting but once you have started the formality of these steps can be relaxed and the whole approach seems more natural. If you itemized the steps involved in boiling an egg it would probably sound just as daunting but, once you have boiled a few eggs, your dependence on steps as such fades. You probably never think of egg boiling as a series of steps ever again. Exactly the same applies to the BMod technique: after some practice the steps fuse together.

Initially the most difficult part of the BMod approach is undoubtedly the novelty of concentrating solely on the external events that surround someone's behaviour. It seems more natural (because it is a more familiar way of thinking about people's behaviour) to slip into speculations about underlying motives, attitudes, and feelings. As I said earlier, BMod doesn't deny the existence of such things. It merely recommends that you solve the problem by changing the external circumstances in which the behaviour occurs.

How Susan and Joy solved their problems

Now that the BMod problem-solving approach has been introduced the time has come to demonstrate how it works in practice by showing how Susan and Joy applied the eight BMod steps.

The solutions they arrived at are not the only ones, in the sense that they are indisputably correct. I have already been careful to point out that there are always a whole host of potential solutions to any personal problem. You may be able to think of 'better' solutions for both problems, but in BMod we are not striving for a perfect or elegant solution; merely for a feasible solution that the problem owner can and wants to use. Both Susan and Joy successfully used these solutions. If the eight-step approach helps you to think of even better solutions then that's splendid – it underlines the flexibility of the BMod approach.

The case of the chauvinistic husband (see page 41)

Step 1   Define the problem behaviour

In broad terms we know that Susan's problem is that Ed is behaving chauvinistically. This covers a multitude of sins including coming home late, never inquiring about Susan's day, commenting if everything isn't 'just so' and lending a hand with ill grace. The secret here is not to be too greedy. The massive problem of Ed being chauvinistic will have to be tackled bit by bit. Susan decided to start with the problem of Ed not helping sufficiently with household chores.

Step 2   Identify the events that trigger Ed's reluctance to lend a hand

Obviously Susan's return to work and all the attendant hassle is a major trigger but we need to be more specific about what events trigger Ed's reluctance to help with household chores. After some probing it became obvious that Susan's manner was the key. When Susan explicitly asked Ed to do something he obliged. If she just 'huffed and puffed' her way around him, grumbling and making oblique comments, he refused to take the hint and lend a hand.

Step 3   Identify the effects that result from Ed's reluctance to lend a hand

An obvious effect for Ed is that he has to do less. We can imagine that the household chores are far from stimulating; Ed is therefore avoiding or minimizing his involvement in essentially tedious chores. (Longer term he may hope that his non co-operation will cause Susan to give up her job and return to waiting on him hand and foot. This is speculation about his *motive* however, rather than looking to see what immediate effects his unhelpfulness result in.)

Step 4   Define the wanted behaviour

Susan wants Ed to do his fair share of household chores without having to be nagged.

Step 5   Ideas for changed triggers

Once it's clear that Susan's manner triggers Ed's non co-operation a whole host of possibilities become apparent. Susan could increase the number of times she explicitly asks Ed to do something, and reduce her innuendos. It would help if Ed is put in sole charge of specific tasks such as preparing breakfast, doing all the vacuuming, buying heavy or bulky provisions (tins and cereals for example). It would make some job satisfaction a possibility if Ed was given *whole* jobs rather than bits and pieces. Another possibility would be to roster jobs on a week-on, a week-off basis. The risk with this is that it causes the routine to chop and change and this might not help the initial challenge of getting Ed into the routine of helping.

Step 6   Ideas for changed effects·

If the new triggers succeed in getting Ed to do his fair share of chores the old effects are automatically altered. After Ed has helped Susan must reward him by, for example, taking an active interest in his work problems, providing little 'extras' that she knows Ed will welcome. Rows must decrease and sex increase. If Ed slips up and fails to carry out his agreed tasks, unless there are extenuating circumstances, Susan must 'retaliate' by being less co-operative herself.

Step 7   Check the feasibility of the changes

Susan considered that all the changes were feasible. The extra effort involved was a small price to pay for a more co-operative husband.

Step 8   Action

Susan implemented the changes on a completely open basis. She talked the whole thing over with Ed and gained his agreement in principle. He confessed himself happier with the certainty of tasks delegated exclusively to him. Within three weeks Ed was doing chores as a matter of routine. In practice the scheme had some welcome side-effects. Ed became more punctual and started to take an interest in her job. Adverse comments declined and Susan did not have to sacrifice her job.

The case of the sexually harassed secretary (see page 42)

Step 1   Define the problem behaviour

Joy finds the men she works with a pain. They make irritating remarks about her size and shape. Each day she is subjected to a bombardment of sexist remarks, retorts, and jokes.

Step 2   Identify the events that trigger the teasing

There are a number of triggers. The sight of oversized Joy is one. She works in an open-plan office and is, in effect, on constant display to the computer programmers. But there is more to it than Joy's appearance. Innocently Joy often lets slip ambiguous remarks with double meanings and these stimulate the sexist retorts. A ray of hope is that Joy notices that the teasing comes from a particular group of male programmers. Even they do not tease her *all* the time (even though it seems like it to Joy). If, for example, they are briefing her about some typing for an important report or if their mutual boss is present or within earshot, the teasing is absent.

Step 3   Identify the effects that result in the programmers' teasing

They get a kick out of it because Joy reacts. The case tells us she invariably blushes or swears at them. Every now and again she gets really upset and breaks down in tears.

Step 4   Define the wanted behaviour

Joy desperately wants to have normal, business-like relations with the male programmers.

Step 5   Ideas for changed triggers

Joy has many possibilities to consider. She could change her job to one where men were in the minority. She could slim! She could ask her boss to partition her office or provide rubber plants to screen her. Two more feasible ideas are for Joy to train herself never to say 'it' and secondly, to give preferential treatment to programmers who are polite and do not tease. She could ensure that their typing is done first for example.

Step 6   Ideas for changed effects

Joy must establish a clear contrast between the service she gives when she is teased and when she is not. When teasing is absent she must produce their work by, or before, the deadline. When they tease she must postpone the completion of their work by moving it to the bottom of the work in hand. Preferably there will be some visible obvious way to do this. She could have all current work listed on a wall board, for example, and when teased simply get up and alter the order. This would also give her something to do and thus reduce the likelihood of blushing and getting upset.

Step 7   Check the feasibility of the changes

Joy rejected the idea of changing her job. She said she would try to slim but sounded halfhearted about it. She introduced the preferential work system, and was ruthless about moving teasers' work to the bottom of the pile.

Step 8   Action

Joy didn't announce any of the changes – she just did them. Each time she moved a piece of work down on her board she explained why in a I'm-having-no-nonsense-from-you way. She thought of some additional changes too. Small things such as not leaving a typewriter cover on at night and being careful to lock all her drawers. This cut down on the pornographic photographs. Gradually the teasing waned, and while it never completely ceased, within a few weeks Joy had reduced it to a tolerable level.

Characteristics of BMod solutions to problems

You will probably have noticed the BMod solutions to personal problems have some characteristic features. The whole approach focuses attention on the events surrounding problem behaviours rather than deeper-seated personality traits. The analysis frequently exposes the problem owner as the unwitting cause of the problem. In any event the approach always invites them to take the initiative in implementing changed circumstances designed to solve the problem.

5

Practical Tips And Your
Questions Answered

This chapter expands on the bare bones of the BMod approach by giving you some practical tips and points to watch for. There are some important principles that should be adhered to. Experts, such as behaviour therapists and psychologists, are careful to employ BMod in a responsible, ethical fashion. It is equally important, if not more important, for you to do the same.

Also in this chapter I deal with some of the reservations you might have about BMod. You may have doubts about the cool, analytical way BMod tackles personal problems. Naturally I'm keen to dispel such doubts and encourage you to use BMod successfully.

Let's start with some practical tips.

Acknowledge people's feelings

BMod does not deny the existence or the importance of underlying factors such as motives, attitudes, or feelings. It does however, strongly recommend that you solve personal problems with other people by focusing on external rather than internal factors. This should not prevent us from identifying with other people's *feelings*. Even though we are powerless to change other people's feelings (only they can do that) there is no reason why we should not put effort into inquiring about them and giving them appropriate acknowledgement.

Empathy, the ability to put yourself in someone else's shoes, is never out of place in BMod. Take Susan's problem with Ed for example. Empathy would help her identify the effects of Ed's behaviour *from his point of view*. She would see how his chauvinism caused her to work even harder, thus making things more convenient for him. Similarly Joy would be in a better position to

57

crack her problem if she could see that the more she shows embarrassment the more she actively encourages the teasing.

Remember however, that empathy on its own changes nothing. It helps us to be 'in touch' and to make sympathetic noises but the only way to solve the problem is to change the circumstances surrounding the behaviour.

Be open

There is no question that BMod works best if you are able to be completely candid with the problem person. More specifically, being open about BMod involves declaring

the problem as you see it
your analysis of why it occurs
your proposals for tackling the problem.

Sometimes an honest declaration of these three things is enough to jolt the problem person into making the necessary changes unaided. In this case the BMod solution remains in the wings ready to come on at a moment's notice. More often a frank declaration results in a temporary improvement with an eventual lapse back into the old way of behaving. This is only to be expected, of course, if the triggers and effects remain unaltered.

However, by far the most likely reaction to an open disclosure of BMod is wry amusement! More often than not the problem person is intrigued with the ingenuity of it all and impressed that you are prepared to go to such lengths to change some aspect of their behaviour. Even chauvinistic Ed professed himself happier with the changes Susan proposed. Joy, on the other hand, had good reasons for not declaring her BMod plan since she was afraid that to do so in advance would provoke even more ridicule. She did, however, openly explain why she was moving a piece of work down the list.

I always encourage people to be open about their intentions and have never known it backfire or cause BMod plans to be abandoned. So please don't imagine that BMod has to be done on a furtive, clandestine basis in order for it to work. Changes to triggers and/or effects will inevitably lead to changes in behaviour irrespective of whether the problem person has been taken into your confidence. Declaring yourself cannot do any harm. Often it aids and abets the process of change. 'Going public' also increases your commitment to go through with it.

'Here and now'

Undoubtedly people acquire their behaviour patterns over a long period of time. This means that everyone's behaviour, unless it is their first attempt at something entirely new, has a history. Accordingly, many approaches are keen to go *backwards* from the current situation to trace the origins of the problem behaviour. In psychoanalysis for example, the aim is to understand what is happening today, however irrational it may seem, by uncovering how the behaviour originated.

BMod, however, whilst acknowledging that all behaviour has a past history, finds it more useful to concentrate on understanding the current triggers and effects. The reason for this is quite simply that we cannot do anything to change what has happened in the past. Our only practical option is to focus on what is happening now, and to work out how to change it in the future. Past history helps us understand why someone persists in using a behaviour we consider strange but it does nothing to help us solve the problem.

Don't generalize

BMod excels at producing tailormade solutions to personal problems. The basic formula is always the same – triggers, behaviours, and effects – but the detail varies from problem to problem. This is inevitable because everybody is unique. While there are many similarities between people, in appearance as well as in personality, it is the differences that count. The approach invites us to be specific about the behaviour, the triggers and the effects. Ed's chauvinism was broken down into a number of behaviours and Susan settled on the specific problems of Ed not helping sufficiently with household chores.

The fact that BMod generates specific, tailormade solutions means that it is handicapped when it comes to producing 'cure-alls'. The fact that Susan successfully solved her problems with her chauvinistic husband is no guarantee that you can take her solution and apply it with equal success to cure your chauvinistic husband. You might pick up some useful ideas but even they will need to be adapted when you incorporate them into your solution.

Be consistent

When we search for triggers and effects in BMod we are looking for links between events that have occurred consistently enough to be apparent. Ed was consistently more chauvinistic after Susan had gone out to work than he had been before this event. The link was fairly apparent. Joy was consistently teased after she had innocently let slip a remark with a double meaning.

The BMod approach is totally dependent upon the discovery of links between behaviour and events. In essence the approach works by breaking old links and establishing new ones. Forging links between triggers, behaviours, and effects is only possible if we are sufficiently consistent and stick unswervingly to our plan. Consistency is particularly crucial if the link between behaviour and its effects is to be established. People are not able to 'discover' that certain behaviours lead to 'nice' consequences unless the pattern repeats itself sufficiently. How could it ever dawn on the programmers in Joy's office that the way to get their work done ahead of schedule was to resist the temptation to tease unless Joy consistently juggled the priorities of her work in hand?

Use short-term effects

Another important principle that helps to establish links between behaviour and ensuing events is to do with the passage of time. The closer in time the effects occur after the behaviour the easier it is for the vital links to become established. If Joy blushed an hour after someone teased her, it is unlikely that the programmers would have developed the habit of teasing Joy in the first place. They acquired this behaviour because Joy immediately showed her embarrassment. The time lapse between their behaviour and its effect on Joy was only a matter of seconds.

The same principle applies when Joy implements her plan to combat the teasing. If, after she has been teased, Joy waits until the next day before she moves a piece of work to the bottom of her work in hand list then the long time lapse will make it extremely unlikely that the teaser will see any connection between the two events. Teasing will therefore continue unabated.

The necessity of having behaviour and effects close together in time may seem obvious and yet it is surprising how often we are careless about applying this principle. BMod reminds us that short-term effects are far more influential than long-term ones.

Effects don't need to be continuous

The need for consistency and for short-term effects may seem rather daunting. If so, you will be glad to hear that effects do not have to follow behaviour every time it occurs. It goes without saying that they must happen frequently enough for the links to be established, but that does not necessarily mean every single time.

The fact that effects still work on an intermittent basis frees us from the considerable burden of ensuring they happen each time the behaviour has occurred. In the initial stages of using a BMod strategy, when first establishing the vital links, it is advisable to discipline yourself to apply the planned effects every time. Once the new behaviour has established itself, continuous effects can gradually be relaxed and give way to intermittent effects.

In practice, therefore, once Susan has Ed trained to lend a hand as a regular, unremarkable routine she need not be so fussy about doing 'extra' things for Ed. She must not, however allow herself to lapse back to the original situation otherwise the carefully established linkages will be broken, with the risk that Ed's chauvinism would reappear. The same applies to Joy. Once the teasing subsides Joy can relax her manipulation of the work in hand but never to the extent that it is altogether abolished.

Use rewards more than punishments

It won't have escaped your notice that in each of the cases we have seen the ideas on changed effects contain both 'carrot and stick'. 'Carrots' are conditional upon the wanted behaviour and 'sticks' are conditional upon the problem behaviour. Susan, therefore, rewards Ed when he has lent a hand and retaliates when he does not. Joy gives work from non-teasers priority over work from teasers. The whole idea is to use rewards and punishments *in combination* as a way of getting a noticeable contrast between 'nice' and 'nasty' effects. Nice effects follow the wanted behaviour, nasty effects follow the problem behaviour. This combination is not absolutely essential. BMod would still succeed in changing behaviour if you concentrated solely on rewarding the wanted behaviour or on punishing the problem behaviour. It does, however, tend to take longer to bring about the desired changes if you depend solely on one or the other. A combination helps break the old linkages and create new ones faster.

A word of warning however. Be extremely careful about the use of punishment. There are two well-known snags with punishment. First, it does not remove problem behaviours so much as temporarily suppress them. Many investigations have shown how a punished behaviour tends to recur once the punishment ceases. The second problem with punishment is that it tends to produce unwanted side-effects. The punished person is likely to harbour some resentment and to scheme their revenge. Remember that rewards are potent enough to influence behaviour even on an intermittent basis. By contrast, punishments are weak enough to require continuous application.

A final word

Always remember that the very essence of BMod is its concentration on *external* events, and not internal motives, attitudes, or feelings.

So much for practical tips. Let me finish this chapter by trying, through a question and answer format, to remove any doubts you might still have about BMod.

If I use BMod will I be accused of being manipulative?

Not if you use it properly. The whole idea of BMod is to modify people but not to manipulate them. As we have already seen BMod is being done openly rather than furtively. The aim is not to exploit people or to trick them into doing something they don't wish to do. Quite the contrary, BMod is at pains to ensure that it is worth people's while to change. Both the problem owner and the problem person stand to gain. Susan benefited by having a husband who was more helpful, but Ed also gained from the new arrangements. He was delegated whole jobs to do and gained from having a more enthusiastic, lively wife who took an interest in his problems rather than being exhausted by coping with her own. Similarly, Joy benefited from less teasing but the programmers in the office also benefited by having their work done on or before schedule.

BMod is not designed to be one-sided. Despite this, it is difficult to see how to make BMod immune from misuse. In unscrupulous hands it can, of course, be used to manipulate. BMod, like any other technique, is neutral. It is the purpose to which it is put that determines its ethics.

If you use BMod as an open and honest attempt to modify people whose behaviour is causing you problems no one will accuse you of manipulation.

If I use BMod will I be solving the real problem or just tinkering about with its symptoms?

You may feel that the emphasis BMod places on the external causes of behaviour makes it superficial and doubt that it is capable of producing permanent solutions to personal problems.

Obviously human behaviour is complex and is caused by a mixture of internal and external factors. Neither enjoys a monopoly when it comes to explaining why people behave as they do. Ed's chauvinism had external and internal causes; Susan starting a full-time job was an external cause and Ed's feelings of annoyance were an internal cause.

The external causes of behaviour are just as real as its internal causes and it is an oversimplification to assume that people's behaviour is exclusively caused by internal thoughts and feelings.

By concentrating on external happenings BMod is being practical but not superficial. External events are the key to understanding and altering people's behaviour.

Might BMod make matters worse rather than better?

Sometimes people object that BMod is dangerous in the sense that 'a little knowledge is a dangerous thing'. They worry that the ordinary lay person is going to be out of their depth with BMod; that it is best left to the experts.

You are much more likely to be out of your depth if you wrestle with intangible aspects, such as motives, attitudes, and feelings, than you are with outward behaviour. Identifying the links between triggers, behaviours, and effects may not be straightforward in every case but even if you failed things would remain unaltered rather than made worse. Even if you got it all wrong and implemented an ill-conceived plan you would know at once when it failed to bring about the desired behaviour.

Realistically, I think there is a slender risk that BMod might trigger a worse behaviour than you started with – if it did you would obviously abandon your plan and think again. It is much more likely that your plan would make no impact whatsoever in which case you would still have the original problem and be no worse off. This would make you realize you must have done something wrong and make you think again.

All things considered, the likelihood of creating a mess is not very great, much smaller in fact than the danger of thoughtlessly creating personal problems in the first place. Certainly the BMod steps are not foolproof, but at least they encourage us to be more thoughtful than we might otherwise be. The alternative is to continue thrashing around on an entirely spontaneous, hit or miss basis. BMod reduces the danger of mishandling our relationships with people by providing an excellent framework. It is not risk free – but then nothing worthwhile ever is.

Will I have the time and patience to use BMod?

When you are suffering from a personal problem things seem urgent and pressing. You want a solution right away and will go to almost any lengths to get one. In these circumstances BMod may seem unduly ponderous and not really quick enough.

BMod is not magic. It might take a number of weeks to reduce the problem behaviour and increase the wanted behaviour. The actual time it takes depends to a large extent on how often you are able to repeat the new triggers and effects. Both Susan and Joy had daily contact with the people they were trying to change. Clearly if, in the normal course of events, you have daily contact with your problem person you are able to repeat the BMod changes more frequently in a shorter period of elapsed time. It is the *frequency* of the trigger-behaviour-effect pattern that counts. Every repetition helps to forge the vital links between the new way of behaving and the new triggers and effects. So while you may need patience during the implementation of your BMod plan you are unlikely to need to invest much, if any, extra time.

The time it takes to carry out the actions involved in introducing changes, triggers, and effects may only amount to a few moments. Neither Susan nor Joy were required to do anything time-consuming in order to solve their problems.

As for the business of going through the BMod steps, I have timed people and on average it takes about forty-five minutes. This is not by any stretch of the imagination a long time – particularly if you consider it in the context of the time wasted directly and indirectly by the personal problem.

While BMod might at first sight seem time-consuming, in actual practice it isn't. In fact, you actually stand to gain time rather than lose it. After all, if the plan you decided on was too time-consuming you would reject it as impracticable and look for something more feasible. Also, with familiarity, the BMod steps take even less time than the average forty-five minutes.

Isn't BMod just common sense?

If people said BMod was common sense without the 'just' I would welcome it as a compliment. After all the dictionary says common sense is 'practical good sense and judgement'. Unfortunately when people say BMod is *just* common sense they obviously mean it to be dismissive. What they are really implying is that the BMod technique has nothing more to offer than the common sense that ordinary people use hundreds of times each day in the normal course of living.

I have already admitted the BMod is not used to produce earth-shattering, novel solutions to personal problems. Nor does it boast any gimmicks or razzmatazz. The test of whether it is just common sense is to see how often it succeeds in getting people to do things it would not otherwise occur to them to do. In my experience BMod scores well. These are just some of the 'unnatural' activities BMod stimulates:

facing problems squarely rather than ducking them or blaming other people for them

66

breaking large problems down into manageable 'bits'

concentrating on outward behaviour rather than getting bogged down with personality factors

concentrating on the 'here and now' rather than being side-tracked into past history

identifying the external events that cause and sustain the problem

working out what to change

taking initiatives to solve the problem

changing yourself in order to change other people

being 'open' with the problem person

being thoughtful and rational about the problem rather than thoughtless and emotional.

Ten plus points, all of which you can say are common sense, but not *just* common sense! The plain fact is that most people do not do any of these things when faced with difficult personal problems, even though there is widespread acceptance that they make sense. Knowing it makes sense and doing it are two quite different things.

6

Some Case Studies And Their Solutions

This chapter gives further examples of the BMod way to solve personal problems of various kinds. Once again, all the problems are drawn from real life and in each case the solutions were successfully put into action.

There are a total of seven cases but there is no need to read them all. It is best just to select one or two for careful scrutiny and just skim through the others. Obviously cases that describe circumstances close to your own will probably catch your attention more readily than those that seem unfamiliar. The important thing is to check that you understand how BMod works sufficiently well to apply the eight-step approach to your own personal problems. To assist this process each of the cases in this chapter follows the eight-step format.

The case of the fractious toddler

Matthew is just three years old and drives his mother scatty. He has frequent outbreaks of fretful and prolonged crying. As a tiny baby he rarely slept through the night and Judy got into the habit of taking him into her bed for a cuddle. (That way at least she got *some* sleep.) Now the nights are less of a problem but Matthew tends to have tantrums at the least provocation. This is particularly irritating because Judy does piece-rate work at home making Christmas crackers. Matthew always seems to kick up a fuss just as Judy settles down to do a stint on the dining-room table. Judy does her best to ignore him but eventually she has to succumb and have him up on her lap. As you can imagine, this seriously interferes with her productivity. (Now you know why you get so many empty Christmas crackers!) Sometimes she loses her temper and gives him a smack – but this always results in even

68

more fractious screaming. Judy is at her wits' end to know what to do.

Step 1 Define the problem behaviour

Judy is being driven scatty by Matthew's tantrums. The case describes his tendency to fretful, prolonged crying which escalates to fractious screaming when Judy loses her temper and smacks him.

Step 2 Identify the events that trigger Matthew's tantrums

The case says he does it 'at the least provocation'. In particular he does it 'just as Judy settles down to do a stint (of Christmas cracker-making) on the dining-room table'. This trigger makes sense because we know there is a history of Matthew crying to win Judy's attention (she used to take him into her bed for a cuddle).

Step 3 Identify the effects that result from Matthew's tantrums

The case describes how 'Judy does her best to ignore him but eventually she has to succumb and have him on her lap'. We can imagine that Matthew finds it a great deal more interesting playing with Judy's Christmas cracker bits and pieces than down on the floor with his own toys. This is confirmed by the fact that if Judy ignores or smacks him the crying doesn't stop but becomes worse.

Step 4 Define the wanted behaviour

No surprises here! Judy obviously wants Matthew to let her do uninterrupted stints of Christmas cracker making.

Step 5 Ideas for changed triggers

There are a number of different changes to consider: Judy could change the *place*. At present Judy does her Christmas cracker making on the dining-room table. The dining room was a separate room off the hall. As far as Matthew was concerned Judy used to vanish leaving him with the run of the kitchen, hall and living room. If Judy moved her Christmas cracker-making to the kitchen table or to a table in the living room it might help. She would no longer 'vanish', and therefore be completely visible to Matthew throughout.

Alternatively, Judy could change the *time*. At present Judy tends to make Christmas crackers in the afternoons *after* mornings spent doing a combination of housework and playing with Matthew. This means that Matthew has all morning to get used to his mother's attention and objects when it is abruptly withdrawn in the afternoon. A better plan would be for Judy to rearrange her day so that Christmas crackers are made in the morning first thing after breakfast leaving the remainder of the day for chores and Matthew.

Another possibility is to change Matthew's activity. Instead of leaving Matthew to his own devices Judy will have to give him something to do. An obvious idea would be to give him his own Christmas cracker-making kit so that he can busy himself with it while Judy gets down to the serious stuff.

Finally Judy could change the length of the 'stint'. At present Judy is lucky to get a maximum of fifteen uninterrupted minutes. She should aim to lengthen this gradually. First to twenty minutes then by additional ten minute increments up to a maximum of fifty minute stints. Eventually it should become 'routine' to take a ten minute break after fifty uninterrupted minutes to play with Matthew.

In real life Judy made all these changes. Her biggest surprise was to find that changing the place and time of day made such a difference.

Step 6   Ideas for changed effects

If Matthew has left her uninterrupted by tantrums or anything else for a 'stint' (initially twenty minutes, then thirty, then forty, then fifty) Judy breaks off to give her undivided attention to Matthew for ten minutes. She plays with him, admires *his* Christmas crackers, has him up on her lap to show him the ones she has made, reads him a short story and so on.

If, on the other hand, Matthew interrupts her before the end of a 'stint', the ten minute play period is withdrawn. She does not succumb and have him up on her lap. She still takes a break but busies herself with making a cup of coffee, tidying the kitchen – doing anything provided she withholds her attention from Matthew.

Step 7   Check the feasibility of the changes

Judy considered she could implement all the changes and certainly thought them worth a try if it would cure Matthew's tantrums and allow her more time to produce the Christmas crackers.

Step 8   Action

It took Judy four weeks to work up to fifty minutes of uninterrupted Christmas cracker production. In the fifth week she managed two fifty minute periods each week-day morning. A dramatic change from snatched, clandestine fifteen minute stints and the irritation of Matthew's temper tantrums.

The case of the defiant teenager

Sara is fourteen years old and seems to go out of her way to defy her parents. If they ask her to do something you can be sure she'll do the opposite, or become stubborn and difficult. In the last week, for example, she has refused to tidy her room, had one of her ears pierced (in deliberate defiance to her father who had expressly forbidden it), used obscene language when told to go to bed and returned later than stipulated from a roller-disco.

Sara's mother takes these things fairly calmly hoping it is a temporary phase. Sara's father, however, becomes very upset and rises to the challenge by losing his temper, forbidding her to go out again, stopping her pocket money and applying similar sanctions. All, it seems, to no avail. Sara's mother has noticed that the defiance increases when her husband is at home. His job, as a company auditor, means he is often away from home during the week but always home over the weekend.

Step 1   Define the problem behaviour

Sara's parents (especially her father) are annoyed by Sara's deliberate defiance. The problem is she does the opposite to what she is asked.

Step 2   Identify the events that trigger Sara's defiance

The case says that Sara does the opposite whenever her parents ask her to do something and that this increases when her father is involved. Reading between the lines you can probably imagine how Sara's parents do their asking. The case mentions words like 'forbid', 'told', and 'stipulated', Sara's father in particular seems to be operating purely on a punitive basis. It mentions his loss of temper and use of sanctions.

Step 3   Identify the effects that result from Sara's defiance

Undoubtedly Sara's defiance is her, very successful, way of gaining her parents – especially her father's – attention. At first sight this may seem a bit kinky but I suspect that when she is being 'good' her father probably ignores her. If he only takes notice of her when she defies him, it is predictable that defiance will increase and compliance decrease.

Step 4   Define the wanted behaviour

Sara's parents want Sara to do what she is asked.

Step 5   Ideas for changed triggers

If there is a significant difference in Sara's defiance depending on whether Sara's mother or father do the asking, one possibility would be to arrange things so that Sara's mother always does it. A better idea would be to change the way they ask Sara to do things and to reserve it for important requests rather than squandering it on relatively minor matters. Telling, forbidding, stipulating, and issuing ultimatums will have to stop since they only trigger Sara's defiance. Instead Sara's parents will have to ask, suggest, negotiate, and compromise. Also, they must be careful to reserve their requests for significant issues. They could clarify this by drawing up a list of all the things they wish Sara would do, putting them into priority order and only 'asking' when the top 25 per cent crop up.

Step 6   Ideas for changed effects

If Sara's defiance is her way of securing attention, albeit disapproving, then the way to change the existing effects is obvious. Sara's parents, especially her father, must be careful to pay her more attention when she does what she is asked than they do when she doesn't do as she is asked. They could try praise, congratulations, treats, pocket money bonuses, and so on. The attention will have to be tailor-made to ensure it is genuinely welcomed by Sara.

By contrast, when Sara is defiant and does the opposite of what she is asked her parents must ignore her. No sanctions, no tantrums, no rising to the challenge – just nothing. This way Sara gets the attention she craves when she is agreeable and gets none when she is defiant.

Step 7   Check the feasibility of the changes

Sara's parents decided to alter the way they asked Sara to do things and to reserve it for important issues. They rejected the idea of confining the asking to one parent. The changed effects were adopted lock, stock, and barrel.

Step 8   Action

Sara's parents chose to tell Sara in a matter-of-fact way what they had planned. Sara could see that it had significant advantages over the old regime. The plan worked with great success. In a few weeks Sara's deliberate defiance had virtually disappeared and Sara's parents were less bothered about things that did not really matter.

The case of the chatterbox neighbour

Jill is plagued by a neighbour who simply will not stop talking. They live on an open-plan estate so escape isn't easy! As soon as Jill steps out of the house her neighbour, a well-meaning middle-aged lady, pounces and starts talking nineteen to the dozen. This happen when Jill puts the baby out in the pram, when she cleans the front doorstep, even when she brings the milk in. The subjects vary from the weather to complaining about the local council to any topical item of news. The talking seems impossible to stop. The neighbour chatters on affably regardless of whether Jill joins in or not. In fact, the neighbour seems oblivious to Jill's signals that she wants to depart. She has tried saying nothing, making excuses that she has left the kettle on, and backing away.

Jill's husband says she'll just have to be rude but Jill wishes there was some other way to curb her neighbour's incessant chatter.

Step 1   Define the problem behaviour

Jill is inconvenienced by her neighbour who 'pounces' and 'will not stop talking'.

Step 2   Identify the events that trigger the neighbour's chatter

This happens 'as soon as Jill steps out of the house'. Obviously the *sight* of Jill outside the front of her house is sufficient to trigger the chattering.

Step 3   Identify the effects that result from the neighbour's chatter

From the neighour's point of view Jill is a handy captive audience. She is someone convenient to talk to, or rather *at* since it is not necessary for Jill to join in! The very fact that Jill stands there, apparently listening to the incessant chatter, is a sufficiently rewarding effect for the neighbour.

Step 4   Define the wanted behaviour

On reflection Jill decides that she does not necessarily want to stop the chatter so much as regulate when it happens so that it no longer inconveniences her.

Step 5   Ideas for changed triggers

Obviously it is not possible for Jill never to step out of the house and open-plan regulations rule out the erection of a six foot high close-boarded fence. Bearing in mind that she wants to regulate *when* the neighbour chatters rather than abolish it, Jill's best plan is to have a standing arrangement whereby the neighbour is invited for coffee say, each Monday and Friday at a specific time. If she wishes Jill can then carry on around her neighbour rather than standing helplessly outside. When her neighbour pounces Jill should grab the initiative by walking briskly towards her saying, 'I'm looking forward to seeing you on Monday/Friday. Sorry I can't stop now. See you on . . .' It would also help to establish regulated encounters if, two or three times a week, Jill goes to the neighbour's front door on a specific mission (to borrow sugar, the local paper, some eggs – anything provided it is specific). This would help Jill become more purposeful in her dealings with her neighbour and the neighbour would start getting used to organized, shorter encounters with Jill.

Step 6   Ideas for changed effects

Under the new arrangements the old effects remain largely intact. Jill is still someone to talk to. The advent of prearranged meetings means that the neighbour can even look forward to a good old natter. Who knows, she may even save up some worthwhile gossip that genuinely interests Jill. Because Jill is better prepared she is also likely to give better value to her neighbour with enhanced effects.

If and when the neighbour reverts to spontaneous pouncing and chattering Jill merely cancels the next arranged meeting and is careful to go out.

Step 7   Check the feasibility of the changes

Jill decided to give it a try. She settled on Tuesdays and Thursdays at eleven for the scheduled visits from her neighbour. When her neighbour first failed to fit in with the new arrangements Jill was apprehensive about cancelling the next meeting but found it surprisingly easy in practice – 'Oh by the way I'm afraid I've got to go out on Thursday so we'll have to miss our little natter. I look forward to catching up on all the news next Tuesday'.

Step 8   Action

Jill decided not to confide in her neighbour. She preferred to use the changed arrangements without drawing attention to them. It all worked like a charm. Within two weeks the neighbour's spontaneous chattering had been cut by half. Within four weeks the problem had been completely overcome.

The case of the sarcastic teacher

Katie is fifteen years old and goes to her local comprehensive school. It's large, with over a thousand pupils, boys and girls. The pupils are banded into four different ability streams, and Katie is at the top of the B stream. She is an extraverted, good-looking girl, very popular with her peers and with the staff.

Unfortunately, her form mistress for the year has a reputation for being one of the more unhelpful members on the staff. Mrs Blithe teaches history but Katie and her class come into daily contact with her in her capacity as their form mistress. The first half hour each morning is a class period before they split up for different lessons with different teachers. The class period is used for a variety of administrative and general purpose activities, and, after only two or three weeks under her jurisdiction, Katie and her classmates have formed a poor impression of Mrs Blithe. They complain that she is disorganized, slow to learn their names, fails to structure the class periods adequately (other teachers lead current affairs discussions, have general knowledge

76

quizzes, and so on), and, above all, that she is sarcastic. Nearly all her spontaneous remarks seem 'loaded' and she seems to take pleasure in making people feel small with her sarcastic remarks. If someone is late it's always 'Thank you very much for coming. We've enjoyed waiting for you'. If someone returns to school after a period of absence it's 'Remind me to tell your parents that they can keep you at home for longer next time'.

Katie, being an effervescent type, often bears the brunt of Mrs Blithe's sarcasm. Katie has told her parents about it but has begged them not to take any action because she wants to solve the problem herself. Katie has noticed that Mrs Blithe tends to make sarcatic remarks only to the girls in the class, never to the boys. If boys annoy her she shouts at them. If girls annoy her she is just sarcastic. Katie, and her friends, wonder how they can solve the problem.

Step 1   Define the problem behaviour

Katie and her girl friends are fed up with Mrs Blithe's unhelpful behaviour. She is disorganized, slow to learn their names, fails to structure class periods and, above all, she is sarcastic. Katie decided to see if she could do something about the sarcastic remarks.

Step 2   Identify the events that trigger Mrs Blithe's sarcasm

Katie is clear that Mrs Blithe makes sarcastic remarks whenever girls in the class annoy her. Virtually any departure from routine will trigger a remark: when girls are late, forget their homework, return after an absence. On reflection Katie also realizes that Mrs Blithe's sarcasm is particularly a problem during the daily form periods. It is less of a problem in one of Mrs Blithe's history lessons.

Step 3   Identify the effects that result from Mrs Blithe's sarcasm

After Mrs Blithe has been sarcastic the girls react demurely. They show that the sarcastic remark has hurt their feelings and become more obedient.

Step 4 Define the wanted behaviour

Katie and her friends want to reduce Mrs Blithe's sarcasm and, if possible, to increase the number of authentic, complimentary remarks she makes.

Step 5 Ideas for changed triggers

Katie can see that it is something about the form periods that triggers Mrs Blithe's sarcasm. She wonders what is significantly different about the history lessons. Gradually it dawns on her that Mrs Blithe is especially sarcastic when reacting, off the cuff, to spontaneous events. The form periods, with high administrative and low teaching content, are packed with incidents that trigger Mrs Blithe's sarcasm. Katie sees that if the form periods were structured in some way it would reduce the opportunity for Mrs Blithe to react in this way. She hits on the idea of getting the boys in the class to suggest a series of quizzes in form periods. A roster of quiz topics is drawn up and a different member of the class acts as quiz master each morning.

Step 6 Ideas for changed effects

Whenever Mrs Blithe makes a complimentary remark (they increase rapidly with the introduction of some 'structure' into form periods) the girls smile and are generally helpful and attentive. On the other hand, when Mrs Blithe slips into her sarcasm the girls ignore it and refuse to look at Mrs Blithe for precisely five minutes. They look straight ahead, down at their books, out of the window, but not at Mrs Blithe.

Step 7 Check the feasibility of the changes

Katie and her friends regarded all the changes as entirely feasible given the constraints of a student-to-teacher relationship. They could see that Mrs Blithe would probably welcome their initiative in organizing structured quizzes in form periods.

Step 8 Action

The whole plan went smoothly. The quizzes reduced admin. time and, within a week, the number of compliments had overtaken the number of sarcastic remarks.

The case of the overdemanding acquaintance

Sheila has been through a rough period. She is middle-aged and had to give up her job as a district nurse when her husband became very ill with heart trouble. He is on the mend now after an operation and has just started to return to work. To fill the gap left after she finished work, and to take her mind off morbid things, Sheila started an Open University course and, after six months, is engrossed and finding it very stimulating. Unfortunately, her studies are frequently interrupted by a woman called Elizabeth who lives just round the corner.

Elizabeth has a history of depression, and walks past Sheila's house twice each day on her way to deliver, or collect, her two young children from the local junior school. Four or five times a week she calls in for a chat. It started innocently enough when Sheila's husband was first ill. Elizabeth used to pop in to see if there was any shopping to do, or anything else she could help with. Gradually, however, the help has given way to long, soul-baring sessions from Elizabeth. She suspects her husband is having an affair, that one of her children is dyslexic, that she has cancer of the left breast – you name it, she suspects it. Of course Sheila listens sympathetically but secretly wishes Elizabeth would go away so that she can get on with her course. She feels that she has had quite enough recent troubles of her own, without being burdened with Elizabeth's. But the main problem is that Elizabeth's visits seriously disrupt her plans to study. Having set time aside, it's absolutely maddening to have Elizabeth encroach on it in this unscheduled, haphazard way. Elizabeth seems oblivious of Sheila's growing resentment. She just waltzes in calling 'Coo-ee, it's only me!', and plonks herself down in the kitchen. She even puts the kettle on to make them both a cup of coffee.

Step 1   Define the problem behaviour

Sheila's study time is being disrupted by Elizabeth's unscheduled 'soulbaring' visits.

Step 2   Identify the events that trigger Elizabeth's visits

Clearly Elizabeth tends to call in when she has a problem. Even more revealing, however, is the fact that she visits on her way to or from the local school. On the morning run she calls in *after* delivering her kids to the school. In the afternoon she calls in *before* collecting them. She never calls in with them nor does she come during school holidays.

Step 3   Identify the effects that result from Elizabeth's visits

The effect for Elizabeth is quite simply that Sheila listens sympathetically. She even gets a cup of coffee thrown in!

Step 4   Define the wanted behaviour

Sheila wants to prevent Elizabeth's visits disrupting her Open University work.

Step 5   Ideas for changed triggers

Sheila could put aside half an hour, at nine o'clock and three o'clock each weekday during school term for Elizabeth. When she did not call in it would be regarded as a bonus. A better idea, however, would be to agree Elizabeth's visits in advance. At three o'clock each Monday, Wednesday, and Friday for example. An afternoon slot is preferable to a morning one because it guarantees Elizabeth's departure time to collect her children from school. Since the urgency and intensity of Sheila's Open University work varies depending on when the next deadline for an assignment has to be in the post Elizabeth, without knowing this, cannot judge when it is convenient to call. Sheila could, therefore, use some simple signal, such as a certain curtain being drawn, to indicate that she must not be interrupted.

Step 6   Ideas for changed effects

When Elizabeth makes an agreed, scheduled visit Sheila gives her undivided attention and listens even more sympathetically than usual. If Elizabeth makes an unscheduled visit the reception is cool. Sheila says, 'Oh I didn't realize you were coming today. I'm afraid I can't stop now but I look forward to seeing you tomorrow at three o'clock'. Sheila is careful not to sit down or to start listening.

Step 7   Check the feasibility of the changes

Sheila broached the subject with Elizabeth and together they planned the changes. Three afternoons were designated for scheduled visits and should circumstances make them inconvenient the front bedroom curtains were drawn as a signal to stay away.

Step 8   Action

There were no snags. Elizabeth's inconvenient visits ceased immediately. The sessions they had were more fruitful than before because Sheila no longer felt resentful that her precious time was being frittered away.

The case of the possessive mother-in-law

Rose is being driven mad by her mother-in-law. She lives only six miles away and was widowed just over a year ago. At sixty-eight she is physically fit but has been devastated by her husband's death. She phones at all hours asking Rose's husband if he could pop over to do various jobs about the house and garden. These requests are rarely made in a straightforward way. For example, she'll complain that the dustbins have been left on the pavement, or that she nearly slipped on the stairs because the hall light bulb needs changing.

Rose's husband, Bill, is an obliging fellow and, as often as not, he goes over to tackle the chores. Once there, his mother contrives to keep him as long as possible. She'll prepare a meal and look crestfallen if he says he can't stay to eat it. As soon as Bill has finished the job he came to do she'll mention something else – 'Oh darling, the front door's so stiff I couldn't open it when the postman rang the other day'; 'Just look at my poor hands. I've been trying to cut down the nettles at the back'; 'I didn't sleep a wink last night with the noises of dripping water from the over-flow'; 'I keep tripping over that loose bit in the crazy paving'.

Bill always returns from these visits to his mother feeling resentful. On the one hand he thinks he should lend a hand, but on the other hand, feels exploited after he has succumbed to her emotional blackmail. He is clear that she has got her martyr's act down to a fine art (she had forty-eight years perfecting it with Bill's father), but feels powerless to combat it. Rose has urged him to take a tougher line, but Bill says it wouldn't be fair until she has had longer to get over her husband's death.

Step 1   Define the problem behaviour

Rose and Bill are victims of Bill's mother's highly polished 'martyr's act'. She phones 'at all hours' making indirect requests for Bill's help. Once she has Bill there she uses every trick in the book to keep him as long as possible. Rose and Bill are prepared to help but want her to be less possessive and more independent.

Step 2   Identify the events that trigger the possessiveness of Bill's mother

As jobs pile up, Bill's mother becomes overwhelmed and tele-phones for help. There is a brief respite for two or three days following one of Bill's visits. Significantly there is also a respite after Bill has arranged to visit.

Step 3   Identify the effects that result from the possessiveness of Bill's mother

From her point of view she gets more jobs done and sees her son more frequently and for longer periods as a result of behaving possessively.

Step 4   Define the wanted behaviour

Rose and Bill want Bill's mother to make less frequent but more straightforward requests for help.

Step 5   Ideas for changed triggers

If Bill was committed to going to his mother's house one evening each week the phone calls would very probably get less. Bill could go straight there from work and 'allow' his mother to provide him with an evening meal. Two days beforehand Bill could phone his mother (*he* phones *her*, note) to find out what job she wants him to tackle. This would 'force' Bill's mother to come out into the open with straightforward requests and help Bill to go properly prepared with the right tools, etc.

Step 6   Ideas for changed effects

Bill now has an easy way to change the effects. He completes all the designated jobs, asks for additional ones and stays half an hour or so longer if his mother drops her martyr's act. Innuendos, crestfallen looks and all the rest cause Bill to leave punctually without volunteering anything extra.

Step 7   Check the feasibility of the changes

The brunt of the changes fall on Bill but they do not require him to do anything untoward. The net result should be that he is inconvenienced a great deal less and his mother assisted a great deal more. Bill chose to explain the new arrangements to his mother quite openly, stressing the benefits for them all.

Step 8   Action

The plan worked like a dream (and they all lived happily ever after!). Bill only had to use the sanction of leaving his mother punctually on eight occasions.

The case of the arrogant doctor

Maureen is a young mother with two toddlers. She has never

been particularly robust, and had to go into hospital for a complete rest before the birth of her last child after tests revealed placenta deficiency. Maureen is a bright girl who now regrets that she left school straight after taking some 'O' levels. (Her father was against girls doing 'higher' education.) Her husband is a salesman working largely on commission for a large food manufacturer.

Maureen hasn't been sleeping too well lately and the doctor prescribed some pills, but these make her feel sick and drowsy for most of the day. Maureen's GP is a brusque man who doesn't suffer fools gladly. He tends to 'talk down' to his patients and make it only too obvious if he thinks they are wasting his time with trivialities. With some reluctance, therefore, Maureen makes an appointment and drags herself, with her two toddlers, back to the surgery.

She has to wait, as usual, in the waiting room, getting more and more anxious and doubtful if she should have come. The last time she saw the doctor she finished describing her symptoms by saying 'I can't understand it'. The doctor's retort had been 'Of course you can't', as he dashed off an incomprehensible prescription without a word of explanation.

Eventually her name is called and, full of trepidation, she makes her way to the surgery. The doctor doesn't look up when she enters the room. He just says, in an automatic way, 'Please sit down. I'll be with you in a minute', and carries on writing up the last patient's notes. After a while, still without looking at Maureen, he says, 'Now, what can I do for you?'. Maureen explains her sickness and drowsiness in an apologetic sort of way: 'I know you're busy but . . .' and 'If it's not too much trouble'. The doctor listens, strums his fingers and asks 'What pills are you on at the moment?'. Maureen's mind goes blank as she tries to recall the name on the bottle. (She had meant to bring them, but forgot in the last-minute hassle of getting the kids ready in time to catch the bus.) The best she can do is describe their shape and colour. The doctor consults her card, writes a prescription, and says, 'Right, let's switch you to these. Come back if you have any further problem.' Maureen hears herself asking what the new pills are. The doctor merely says, 'Would you be any the wiser if I told you? Just come back if they don't do the trick. Good day', and pushes the button that signals the next patient. Maureen exits, muttering her thanks.

On her way home Maureen reflects on this latest bruising encounter with her GP. She wonders what's involved in changing her doctor, but imagines she would have to have a more substantial complaint than mere arrogance.

Step 1   Define the problem behaviour

Maureen has problems with her GP's brusque manner. To all accounts he doesn't suffer fools gladly and 'talks down' to Maureen, making it painfully obvious that she is wasting his time. There are many aspects to his behaviour and Maureen must choose what to tackle first. She decides to try to get him to give informative answers to her questions.

Step 2   Identify the events that trigger the doctor's brusque replies

Obviously questions trigger answers so the doctor's lack of response must be something to do with the way Maureen asks her questions. We can imagine she does so in a self-deprecating, apologetic manner, 'I'm sorry to trouble you but . . .' and 'I know you are very busy but . . .'.

Step 3   Identify the effects that result from the doctor's brusque replies

The doctor succeeds in ridding himself of an insignificant, boring patient. He also avoids having to justify or explain his actions.

Step 4   Define the wanted behaviour

Maureen wants informative answers to her questions.

Step 5   Ideas for changed triggers

Maureen needs to change her questioning manner. She should work out, in advance, an assertive way of doing this. When the doctor next hands her a prescription without explanation she should avoid taking it, and say something along these lines: 'When you give me a prescription without an explanation I am less inclined to complete the course of treatment. I feel that you can't be bothered to spend time on me. So, I'd really like you to answer my questions. What is this prescription for and how will it help me to get better?'

Step 6　Ideas for changed effects

When the doctor gives Maureen a satisfactory answer she gives an appreciative smile, thanks him and leaves. If the answer is brusque and unsatisfactory Maureen sits tight either asking further questions or, if her mind goes blank, simply saying, 'Please answer my question, doctor.'

These changes mean that the doctor gets rid of Maureen faster when he answers her questions than when he doesn't. The old state of affairs has been reversed.

Step 7　Check on the feasibility of the changes

You will notice that everything depends on Maureen's ability to project herself assertively. She did this by first changing her underlying feelings of anxiety and fear.

Step 8　Action

Maureen took the precaution of learning her words by heart. The first time she tried it the doctor was incredulous (his mouth dropped open and he even looked at her!). She repeated the formula on her next two visits to the doctor. On the fourth, the doctor volunteered a decent explanation without any probing from Maureen.

7

How To Alter Your Own Behaviour

In this chapter we will see how to use the BMod approach to modify your own behaviour rather than other people's.

The shift away from other people and towards you is deliberate and significant. You are a key figure in all your personal problems. Not only are you the person who decides what to regard as a problem by seeing a gap between what you've got and what you want, but also your reactions largely determine whether the problem goes or stays. We have seen how the person who owns the problem always has it within their power to solve the problem or lessen it. Your actions can create the problem, maintain the problem, make the problem worse, or solve it.

Until now we have concentrated on how you can take certain actions to modify other people's behaviour in order to overcome the problem. The actions you take inevitably mean you have to change in order to bring about the desired changes in other people. Perhaps the best example of this to date is the case of Maureen and her doctor. We saw how the doctor's offhand manner was triggered by Maureen's non-assertive approach and that the solution was largely in Maureen's own hands. By steeling herself to be more assertive in her questioning, she brought about a change in the doctor's manner. The key was for Maureen to change her own behaviour and thus get the desired effect. In different ways all the problem owners have had to make adjustments to their own behaviour in order to bring about changes in other people.

Of course we might want to change some aspects of our own behaviour irrespective of other people. If we are honest with ourselves there are probably lots of behaviours we would like to modify if only we knew how. You might be the sort of person who is quick-tempered and invariably regrets it afterwards. You might have habits that you can't shake off such as smoking or overeating. You might wish you could be the life and soul of the party or be less dogmatic with the children. The possibilities are endless.

If we wished we could apply BMod to ourselves, not just to solve problems but also as a means of self-development. The BMod assumption that behaviour has been largely acquired as a result of a lengthy learning process means that we should be able to unlearn any behaviour we choose and replace it with something new. There is no reason why we should go through life, unless we wish to, sticking doggedly to the same, familiar behaviour patterns. We are free to experiment with new, perhaps totally uncharacteristic ways of behaving. After all if we don't develop ourselves it is most unlikely that anyone else will do it for us. Ultimately we are each responsible for managing our own actions and emotions even though it is often more convenient to pretend otherwise. There are all sorts of excuses for not taking ourselves in hand – obligations to other people, the fact we are too busy just now, the upheaval involved, our lack of willpower and so on. But perhaps the biggest single reason why more people don't develop themselves is that they do not know how to. As we shall see BMod is an excellent framework for self-development and self-management.

The question is how can we change our behaviour be it to solve a problem or develop ourselves? How can we select what behaviour to modify? What are the differences between altering other people and altering ourselves? Is it still a question of identifying and changing triggers and effects? Can it be done without help from a third party?

This chapter answers these questions by showing you how to apply the BMod technique to yourself. Modifying our own behaviour is remarkably similar to modifying someone else's. The eight BMod steps remain basically the same with some essential practical differences when it comes to applying them to ourselves. These differences can best be highlighted if we take a look at each of the BMod steps once again.

Step 1   Be clear and specific about the problem behaviour

It is more difficult to decide which of your own behaviours to modify. When you do this with someone else in mind you are likely to be all too clear about which of their behaviours cause you problems! Trying to identify your own problem behaviour is a tougher assignment. This is because you view your own behaviour from the inside looking out whereas other people's behaviour has to be viewed from the outside only. You find it easier to justify your own behaviour beause you know (or think you know) your motives. You hear people saying 'I did it with the best of intentions' and, of course, that is exactly right. Most of our actions are undertaken with the conviction that we are doing the best thing, with the right motives, in the circumstances.

So how shall we know what to set about changing? Here are some ideas to get you started.

Accept criticisms   When people grumble, complain, nag, and criticize you resist the temptation to rush to your own defence. Instead accept their adverse comments as a point of view worth considering. If possible get them to be *specific* about the behaviour they object to and ask them for actual examples. You are then in a position to mull over the information you have received and decide whether to do anything about it or not.

This may sound like a tall order but it is surprisingly easy to welcome adverse comments so long as you know what to *do* about them. It is when you feel out of your depth and vulnerable that you are likely to become defensive, or even offensive, when people criticize you. The BMod approach is your protection.

Invite information about yourself   You don't have to wait for adverse comments, or even compliments to come to that, you can actively encourage them. It is surprising how rarely this is done when you bear in mind what a valuable source of information other people are. There is nothing easier than to ask someone who knows you well, 'What did you think of that?' It takes a bit more courage to invite comments from comparative strangers but even this can be very worthwhile (sometimes more worthwhile). Again the secret is to invite comments on something specific. Not 'What do you think of me?' but 'How do you think I handled that phone call?' or 'What should I have done when Susan was rude just now? Is there a better way of handling her when she is like that?'

You might hesitate to solicit comments because you think people will resent it. However, asking someone for their opinion is an essentially complimentary thing to do. It shows that you value their views. If you hesitate to ask for information because you fear you might spark off a tirade then remind yourself that it's better to know than to be ignorant about how you appear to other people. You might as well gain from what they have to say.

Pretend you are at fault   Whenever you are disappointed with someone else pretend that your behaviour was the cause. This is grossly unfair because many times you will in fact have been innocent, but the assumption that it was your fault helps you to scrutinize your own actions rather than point the finger at other people. So next time you hear that someone has given a party to which you were not invited don't go all paranoid. Instead ask yourself 'What have I done to be excluded from their guest list?' Or, to give another example, next time someone is rude to you say to yourself 'What did I do to cause that?' The assumption that we are right and other people are always at fault blinds us to many learning opportunities. By standing the assumption on its head we gain insights into how we unconsciously trigger adverse reactions in other people. It also helps us develop a better understanding of their point of view. This does not mean that we have to *accept* that our behaviour is always to blame. The trick is to *pretend* it is as a handy device for self-appraisal.

Admit your weaknesses   In the absence of comments from, and disappointments about, other people you can give yourself information. Most of us have weaknesses that we acknowledge but don't do anything about. You might not be able to rattle them off at the drop of a hat but over a period of time you could compile a list. Anything trivial or serious can go down on the list because you can sort out priorities once it is compiled. Here is an example:

eating too many biscuits between meals
not cleaning teeth with an 'up and down' action
pretending not to notice someone you know
not saying what you really think
being pessimistic
falling asleep in front of the telly
hesitating to phone someone you should
not washing your hands after going to the toilet
biting your nails
eating chocolates compulsively

Notice that the list contains items which could hardly be described as personal problems in the way we have defined them. Not cleaning your teeth properly and failing to wash your hands when you should are not necessarily relationship or psychological problems but they might nevertheless be actions you take (or don't take) frequently enough to cause you disappointment.

Set yourself challenges   The fifth and last idea to get you started is rather different. The previous four ideas have all dwelt on problems, whether they arose from other people or from our own weaknesses list. This is understandable because first and foremost BMod is a problem-solving technique. But if we want to use it as an aid for self-development we need not be confined to problems as such. We could complement our list of weaknesses with a list of strengths for example; actions that we would like to consolidate or use more often. Also we could set ourselves deliberate challenges purely for learning purposes. Challenges usually involve us in departing from a familiar trusted routine. If you use the same route to the shops set yourself the challenge of finding three different ones. If you have a daily routine at work or at home totally change it for one week. If you never write letters write a long newsy letter to a friend each day for a week. If you read the newspaper avidly each day forgo it for a period and write poetry instead. If you normally get up at seven in the morning make it an hour earlier and go for a walk at dawn. If you stick to your familiar set of friends and acquaintances force yourself to strike up a conversation with someone new each day. Wear different clothes. Do your hair differently.

These are only examples. The possibilities are endless. The whole idea is to break free from cosy 'safe' routines and go out on a limb in order to have, and learn from, new experiences. How BMod can help prevent us from becoming set in our ways will become clearer as we progress through the remaining steps.

Step 2 and 3   Identify the events that trigger the behaviour and the effects it results in

I will take these two steps together because the differences in applying them to your own behaviour as opposed to other people's are exactly the same.

The most obvious difference is that you might find it more difficult to step outside yourself and be sufficiently objective in your search for the triggers and effects surrounding your behaviour. They exist but the difficulty is to spot the external events and disentangle them from the accompanying internal thoughts and emotions.

The best tip I can give to help pinpoint triggers is to force yourself to answer the question '*When* do I do such and such?' and keep at it until you have got an answer. I have used this question with great success to reveal many triggers for my own behaviour that I was previously unaware of. Consequently I now know exactly what triggers my headaches, my temper, accidents with my hedgetrimmer, nibbling my nails, drinking too much and having a listless, unproductive day. Knowledge of the external triggers that influence me has given me the option of controlling or abolishing all these reactions.

If answers to the questions are not immediately forthcoming there are two things you can do. One is to try putting the question the other way round by asking yourself 'When don't I do so and so?' Initially the answers might sound daft but if you keep at it you are bound to narrow down the possibilities. I don't lose my temper when I'm asleep for example, nor do I lose it with my clients or patients. I don't lose it with animals but I do lose it with things, such as when wiring plugs or undoing rusty bolts. I don't lose my temper with my wife or children but I do lose it with other people's children; but only when they break or spoil something when visiting my home. And so on. Eventually triggers are bound to emerge. The second thing you can try is a bit more laborious and that is to keep a note of when the behaviour in question occurs. I tracked down the triggers for my headaches by keeping notes in my diary. (It happens whenever I am late, whenever I am confused about my role, when I know my wife is anxious about something, when it becomes obvious that I am not going to achieve my self-imposed targets for the day.) Before keeping notes I had no idea what brought on the headaches or even how often they happened. As soon as I had identified the triggers it became obvious what steps I could take to avoid or at least minimize headaches.

When it comes to identifying your own effects my advice is much the same. Keep asking yourself 'After I have done so and so what's in it for me?' As always try to stick to *external* effects rather than slipping hazily into saying 'It makes me feel better'. Sometimes you must expect to draw a blank and not be able to identify an effect at all. I could never find a positive effect for cutting myself with my hedgetrimmer for example. I am convinced that it was a 'one-off' accident even though I have done it twice in more or less exactly the same circumstances (when I'm up a ladder and at full stretch, hurrying to finish the very last bit of hedge that needs trimming). The sorts of behaviour that have discernible effects are the ones that repeat themselves over and over again. When I lose my temper with rusty bolts for example, it wins sympathy and even offers of assistance from whoever is within earshot. When I lose my temper with other people's children (not that this happens too often!) it causes them to sit up and take notice of me and (at any rate for a short while) to do as I say. It even succeeds in getting the parents of the children to apologize, make good the damage, take their children away, and so on.

Do not give up the search for effects too easily. It is a question of searching to see what happens as a consequence of your behaviour that you regard as 'nice' in some way. Habitual behaviours are bound to have effects that sustain them and encourage their repetition. If, search as you might, you cannot identify a clear effect then by all means ask anyone who knows you well and has witnessed the behaviour in question. They might be able to throw light on your effects. Notes can help too though I have found note-keeping more useful in uncovering obscure triggers.

If having tried all these things you are none the wiser, all is not lost. You can still modify your behaviour by altering the triggers and inserting an 'artificial' effect as a reward. More about this in a moment.

Step 4 Be clear and specific about the behaviour you want

This step remains the same whether you are applying BMod to yourself or someone else. If you are using BMod to get rid of a weakness then the behaviour you want is usually the opposite of what you've got at present. If, on the other hand, you use BMod to develop a behaviour which is already a strength then this obviously won't be an opposite and may require more careful thought at this stage. Suppose, for example, I want to become more accomplished at small talk. I need to be clear what 'more accomplished at small talk' actually means, otherwise I shall not know when I have achieved it and will probably be vague about the triggers and effects to bring it about. I therefore need to be more specific. What is 'small talk'? What is *accomplished* small talk'? How shall I know I have raised my small talk to these giddy heights? It is all a matter of definition. For BMod purposes a precise enough one would be: to sustain a conversation with any stranger on insignificant matters (i.e. no religion, politics, or sex) for at least ten minutes. Being clear and specific about the behaviour you want is an essential requirement before moving on to consider changes to triggers and effects.

Step 5   Work out how to change the triggers so that the problem behaviour is no longer triggered and the wanted behaviour is

There are no changes to this step irrespective of whether you are using BMod on yourself or another person. Success at this stage is very dependent on whether you have been able to pinpoint what triggers the problem behaviour back at step 2. If you have then it is a comparatively simple matter to work out what to change. If I have accidents with the hedgetrimmer when I am up a ladder at full stretch, hurrying to finish the very last bit of hedge that needs trimming, then there are at least three changes that come immediately to mind. One is to move the ladder more frequently so that I never have to reach at full stretch. Another is to go more slowly towards the end of the job when I am getting tired and therefore more accident-prone. A third change would be to split the job into two distinct hedgetrimming sessions with a proper break in between to reduce the risk of hurrying and to make it more likely I was properly rested by the time I got to the last bit of hedge. There are lots of other ideas that come to mind. I could change the ladder so that it was freestanding and less wobbly. I could wear protective gloves whenever I use the hedgetrimmer and so on. All these ideas, and others like them, are sparked by the identification of what triggers the problem behaviour. This is why it is so important to do a thorough analysis at step 2 in the BMod routine.

Step 6   Work out how to change the effects so that the problem behaviour is no longer encouraged and the wanted behaviour is

This is undoubtedly the most difficult of the steps to tackle on a do-it-yourself basis. There are a number of reasons for this. In the first place you may feel uncertain what the existing effects of your behaviour are. To the extent that you had trouble identifying them back at step 3 you are bound to be short of ideas on what to change now at step 6. Secondly, even if you succeeded in identifying the existing effects they are bound by definition to be 'nice' and therefore it is almost masochistic to forgo them. If, whenever I lose my temper, visiting children stop spoiling my things and their parents rush around making good the damage why on earth should I change such a highly effective behaviour? Finally, your effects are, more often than not, rooted in *other people's reactions* to your behaviour, which really means that you need to change them before you can change yourself.

I have two useful tips to make the burdensome task of changing your own effects more manageable. The first is to enlist someone else's help, preferably a key person who is already 'involved' in the sense that their reactions are an integral part of your effects. It might be your spouse, your partner, a relative, friend, or colleague – anyone who has frequent contact with you and so is already involved. It also helps if they stand to gain from the demise of your problem behaviour because it is then to their advantage to help you. If friends and neighbours rally round and obligingly undo rusty bolts for me when they have heard me curse and swear, I need their co-operation to break the existing link between losing my temper and help being proffered. This is a good example of the sort of outside assistance you might require because it illustrates how you need people to withdraw their usual reaction and thus deprive you of your expected effects. Frequently you will find you need to brief people to ignore you when you lose your temper or when you sulk or when you complain of a headache or whatever. This is because an analysis of the effects sustaining many of your bad habits reveals that they are, in various ways, attention-seeking. If people didn't pay any attention to you when you were, say, rude and paid rapt attention to you when you were polite you would be polite more often. Unfortunately in this topsy-turvy world it is usually the other way round: people pay more attention to you when you are rude than they do when you are polite. This is how people learn to be rude.

Getting people to ignore you is one way to break the existing links between your problem behaviour and its effects. However, if you depended solely on this strategy you would have a BMod plan that was based more on measures of punishment than on rewards. Earlier in Chapter 5 (pages 57–67) I suggested that you place more emphasis on positive rewards than on punishments. Of course you might be able to enlist someone's help to the extent that they ignore the problem behaviour when it occurs and reward the right behaviour. This gives them a far more difficult task (making it easier for them to slip up) and delegates too much of your BMod plan. It is better to keep more control over your own plan.

My suggestion is, therefore, that you draw up your own list of positive effects and reward yourself with something from the list each time you succeed in using the wanted behaviour rather than the problem behaviour. This is artificial in the sense that you insert a contrived reward rather than using one that flows more naturally from the behaviour. So, for example, after I have succeeded in not losing my temper, I could reward myself with a slice of chocolate cake, provided of course that I like chocolate cake!

Compiling your own list of rewarding effects is easy. It is just a question of writing down all the things you like doing. They need to be small, everyday things bearing in mind the importance of being able to reward yourself with them immediately after the behaviour rather than longer term. You may like going to the theatre but this should not figure on your list because for BMod purposes it is too big a treat that couldn't be administered frequently enough on a short-term, here-and-now, basis. In this respect slices of chocolate cake are a better idea.

Obviously your list of rewards will have to be personal to you because only you know what you like. I certainly can't suggest items for your list but I can give examples from my own list and from other people's that I have glimpsed. Here is a miscellaneous selection:

playing the piano
doing some knitting/tapestry/sewing
playing space invaders

eating chocolates
going for a jog/swim/cycle ride
having a cup of coffee
going round the garden
chatting to a friend
phoning someone
putting money in a tin
reading the newspaper
looking at a magazine
listening to a favourite piece of music
reading five pages of a favourite book
looking at a favourite picture (photograph or painting)
tending/talking to indoor plants
looking to see what is on television this evening
opening the post
taking the dog for a walk
doing the daily crossword.

The best items for your list are things you enjoy that you can do by yourself in no more than ten to fifteen minutes. Above all the items on the list should be things it is feasible to do very soon after the behaviour in question. Remember though that you do not need to do them every time. You might find it more feasible to reward yourself intermittently.

Once you have compiled your personal reward list it is invaluable not just within the BMod discipline but on any occasion when you want to reward yourself. I have found it useful in combating procrastination, for example. If you are like me you tend to postpone nasty or difficult jobs in preference for the nicer, easier ones. Your list can rescue you from this tendency by operating it on an 'if – then' basis.

Parents already do this with children – 'If you eat your greens *then* you can have some ice cream', 'If you clear up your bedroom *then* I will give you your pocket money'. The 'if – then' formula can just as easily be applied by yourself to yourself. 'If I clean the kitchen *then* I will go round the garden', '*If* I go shopping *then* I will read my book'.

It is amazing how by managing your own effects you can get more done and be more satisfied. These are the longer-term advantages of being skilful at self-management.

Step 7   Check that your plan is feasible and work out how to put it into action

Everything I have said in earlier chapters about having a feasible, practicable BMod plan applies equally when you are applying BMod to yourself. If you cut too many corners and fail to implement your changed triggers and changed effects then it will not work. Inevitably, you will slip back into the old way of behaving unless you have such strong willpower that you can bring about behavioural changes even though the surrounding circumstances remain the same. Some people seem able to do this – and good luck to them. However, for everyone who finds willpower alone inadequate to the task of effecting permanent behaviour changes (and that includes me) I recommend BMod. Your plan must be such that you can keep it up through thick and thin, perhaps for weeks. If you embark on a plan that is fine on paper but unrealistic in practice BMod will be relegated to an interesting academic exercise instead of being the powerful, practical tool for change that it really is.

8

Problem-Solving Forms
To Help You

The whole idea of this book is to help you become self-sufficient in solving your own relationship problems. The next few pages contain a number of personal problem solving forms. They are designed to guide you through the first six steps of the eight-step routine which was first introduced in Chapter 4 (see pages 41–56).

If you get stuck there are two things you can try. One is to refresh your memory about how the BMod steps work by reading through a couple of the cases in Chapter 6. If that doesn't do the trick then you can use the letter at the end of this chapter to write to me about your problem. If you give me all the information I ask for in the letter I should be able to come up with some helpful suggestions. So don't hesitate to post the letter off to me (with a stamped addressed envelope, please) and I shall send a reply back to you.

Good luck in finding lasting solutions to more of your personal problems than ever before!

PERSONAL PROBLEM SOLVING FORM

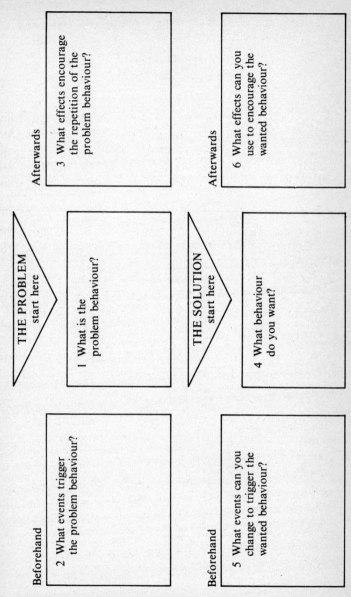

Beforehand

2 What events trigger the problem behaviour?

THE PROBLEM
start here

1 What is the problem behaviour?

Afterwards

3 What effects encourage the repetition of the problem behaviour?

Beforehand

5 What events can you change to trigger the wanted behaviour?

THE SOLUTION
start here

4 What behaviour do you want?

Afterwards

6 What effects can you use to encourage the wanted behaviour?

To: Peter Honey
    Sheldon Press,
    SPCK Building,
    Marylebone Road,
    London NW1 4DU

From: Name ....

Address ....

....

....

Dear Peter Honey,

SOLVING PERSONAL PROBLEMS

I'm sending you this letter because I have a relationship problem of the type
you describe in your book that I can't seem to solve on my own. I hope you
will be able to make some helpful suggestions. Here are my answers to your
questions.

> Who is the problem with? (i.e. husband, friend, neighbour. If it is
> with a child please give age).

> In a single sentence, what is the problem behaviour?

> When does this behaviour occur? What triggers have you been
> able to identify?

What effects result from the behaviour that seem to be encouraging its repetition?.

In a sentence, what behaviour do you *want?* (as opposed to the behaviour you have).

Finally, what have you already tried, or what have you thought of trying, in order to solve the problem?

I enclose a stamped, self-addressed envelope and look forward to your reply.

Yours sincerely,

Index

INDEX